MATH SERIES

Pre-Algebra

COMPANION

For parents and teachers: a straightforward way
to teach and test pre-algebra skills

A Breath of Fresh Air
Garlic Press

Copyright © 2007 Stanley H. Collins
All rights strictly reserved.

Published by
Garlic Press
605 Powers St.
Eugene, OR 97402

ISBN 978-1-9308-2063-0
Order Number GP-163
Printed in China

www.garlicpress.com

TABLE OF

Contents

Introduction

The Pre-Algebra Companion is a focus on skills which extend arithmetic competency and which aid a smooth transition into formal Algebra. It fits all learners who have mastered basic operational and computational skills as well as those proficient in problem solving.

In an era when national standards are so finely focused, the *Pre-Algebra Companion* is aligned with standards and principles to achieve success. *The Pre-Algebra Companion* is organized into twelve chapters. Each chapter is a step-by-step model that presents and explains a new concept, that provides examples, and that provides practice as a measurement of the presentation and explanation. This model is designed for clarity, unencumbered with fillers or distracting graphics. A Mastery Test provides a measurement for retained learning.

The twelve chapters can proceed in sequence, or individual chapters can be used to supplement other, standard texts. Perhaps the two chapters on Exponents may be taken from their present order and presented together. The same may apply to Integers and Rational Numbers. Both focus on signed numbers, with Rational Numbers accentuating manipulation of fractions. Of all the chapters, Variables approaches the symbolic expression so familiar to Algebra.

CHAPTER 1

Order of Operations

When more than one operation is needed to solve a mathematical expression or problem, there is a procedure to be used: **The Order of Operations**. Follow these steps:

1. Solve operations within parentheses
2. Calculate any exponents
3. Solve multiplication or division from left to right
4. Solve addition or subtraction from left to right

Example 1

$30 \div 5 + 25 \cdot 3$	*Step 3 : Reminder – Solve division or multiplication from left to right.*
$6 + 25 \cdot 3$	*Step 3 : Division completed.*
$6 + 75$	*Step 3 : Multiplication completed.*
81	*Step 4 : Addition completed.*

Example 2

$3(8 - 3) - 6 \div 2$	*Step 1 : Solve the operation within parentheses.*
$3(5) - 6 \div 2$	*Step 1 : Remove parentheses.*
$15 - 6 \div 2$	*Step 3 : Multiplication completed.*
$15 - 3$	*Step 3 : Division completed.*
12	*Step 4 : Subtraction completed.*

Example 3

$5^2 + (4 \cdot 5 - 2) \div 9$	*Step 1 : Solve the operation within parentheses.*
$5^? + 18 \div 9$	*Step 1 : Remove parentheses.*
$25 + 18 \div 9$	*Step 2 : Exponent calculated.*
$25 + 2$	*Step 3 : Division completed.*
27	*Step 4 : Addition completed.*

Notice how multiplication in Step 1 takes precedence over subtraction when removing the parentheses. In operation within parentheses, multiplication and division must be performed before addition and subtraction.

EXERCISE 1.1

Use the Order of Operations to solve these problems.

1. $(30 - 3) \div 9$
2. $2 \cdot (3 + 5)$
3. $(7 - 2) + (4 + 3)$
4. $2(12 + 2) - 3(5 - 2)$
5. $3 + 6 - 3^2$
6. $24 + 4^2 - 15$
7. $24 + 6^2 \div 12$
8. $(24 + 6^2) \div 12$
9. $2 + 3(2 + 1) - 2^2$
10. $28 \div 2 + 4$

11. $36 - 5 \cdot 6$
12. $4 - 2 \cdot 3 + 12 \div 2$
13. $36 \div 6 - 15 \div 5$
14. $18 - 4^2 \div 2$
15. $24 \div 3 \cdot 5 - 12 + 5$
16. $7^2 + (3^3 - 14) \cdot 2$
17. $38 - 7 \cdot 4 - 4 \cdot 2$
18. $3(8 + 7 \cdot 4 - 4 \cdot 2)$
19. $12 - 2^2 \cdot 2 \div 4$
20. $(23 - 7) + 2(10 \div 5) - 9$

EXERCISE 1.2

State the operations in order that will solve each problem.

1. $(6 + 3)^2 - 4 \cdot 2$

_____

_____

_____

_____

2. $(25 - 3)(5 + 9)$

_____

_____

3. $25 - 3 \cdot 5 + 4$

_____

_____

_____

4. $16 \div 3 + 12 \cdot 2$

_____

_____

_____

Factors

Factors are quantities (sometimes numbers, sometimes variables) which when multiplied together yield a product.

Example 1

Factors of 14 are :   a. $1 \cdot 14$

b. $2 \cdot 7$

14 has four (4) factors: 1, 2, 7, 14

Example 2

What are the factors of 24?

Answer: $1 \cdot 24$

$2 \cdot 12$

$3 \cdot 8$

$4 \cdot 6$

Example 2 shows combinations of factors, in pairs, that equal 24. From this we can state that the **whole number factors** of 24 are: *1, 2, 3, 4, 6, 8, 12, 24.*

Example 3

Is 12 a factor of 60?

Answer: It is if 12 divides evenly into 60.

$60 : 12 - 5$

12 divides evenly into 60. It divides 5 times.

Yes, 12 is a factor of 60.

EXERCISE 2.1

Factor the products: 1) show factors as pairs; and, 2) list the whole number factors of each product.

1. 10   1) 1 · 10, 2 · 5

                 2) 1, 2, 5, 10

2. 42	**5.** 48	**8.** 110
3. 60	**6.** 25	**9.** 333
4. 16	**7.** 20	**10.** 7

Is the first number a factor of the second? Why? or Why not?

11. Is 7 a factor of 63? Why? or Why not?

12. Is 3 a factor of 117? Why? or Why not?

13. Is 12 a factor of 12? Why? or Why not?

14. Is 4 a factor of 46? Why? or Why not?

15. Is 10 a factor of 130? Why? or Why not?

16. Is 1 a factor of 23? Why? or Why not?

17. Is 24 a factor of 144? Why? or Why not?

18. Is 5 a factor of 151? Why? or Why not?

Circle the numbers that are factors of the first number:

19. 6: 1 2 3 4	**24.** 45: 3 6 9 12
20. 17: 4 9 11 17	**25.** 27: 1 3 9 12
21. 37: 5 6 7 8	**26.** 28: 3 5 7 9
22 20: 1 5 10 20	**27.** 105: 5 25 53 105
23. 30: 3 5 12 15	**28.** 128: 8 32 48 64

CHAPTER 3

Prime and Composite Numbers

Knowledge of factors will help in identifying prime and composite numbers.

Prime numbers: A whole number greater than 1 that has only 1 and itself as factors.

Composite numbers: A whole number greater than 1 that has at least one factor besides itself and 1.

Through a process called **prime factorization**, all composite numbers can be reduced to the product of only prime numbers. A simple representation of prime factorization, illustrating the relationship of prime and composite numbers, is a **factor tree**. Consider these examples:

Example 1

What are the prime numbers (also prime factors) of 6?

Answer: *Composite number*

Step 1: 2 prime numbers:
the only factors of 2: 1 · 2
the only factors of 3: 1 · 3

Example 2

What are the prime numbers of 12?

Answer: 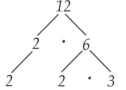 *Composite number*

Step 1: 1 prime number and 1 composite number

Step 2: 3 prime numbers:
the only factors of 2: 1 · 2
the only factors of 3: 1 · 3

Note: In Step 1, use of 3 · 4, instead of 2 · 6, will still yield the same prime numbers in Step 2.

Example 3

What are the prime numbers of 72?

Answer:

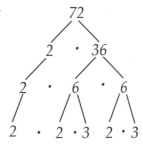

72   Composite number

2 · 36   Step 1: 1 prime number and 1 composite number

2 · 6 · 6   Step 2: 1 prime number and 2 composite numbers

2 · 2 · 3 2 · 3   Step 3: all prime numbers

Formally the prime numbers should be ordered from smallest to largest, such that
72 = 2 · 2 · 2 · 3 · 3.

Note: Step 1 could have been 4 · 18 or 9 · 8 and still have yielded 2 · 2 · 2 · 3 · 3 in Step 3.

EXERCISE 3.1

Use the factor tree to reduce these composite numbers to prime numbers.

1. 81
9 · 9
___ · ___ · ___ · ___

2. 48
6 · 8
___ · ___ · ___ · 4
/ \
___ · ___

3. 225
5 · 45
___ · ___ · ___
/ \
___ · ___

4. 64
4 · 16
___ · ___ · ___ · 4
/ \ / \
___ · ___ · ___ · ___

Complete the factor tree for each problem.

5. 14
2 · ___

6. 21
7 · ___

7. 35
7 · ___

8. 39
3 · ___

Complete the factor tree for each problem and gather the prime factors.

9. 90
3 · ___
___ · ___
/ \
___ · ___

Prime factors =
___ · ___ · ___

10. 88
2 · 44
___ · ___
/ \
___ · ___

Prime factors =
___ · ___ · ___

11. 225
5 · 45
___ · ___
/ \
___ · ___

Prime factors =
___ · ___ · ___

12. 48
___ · 12
___ · ___ · ___ · ___
/ \
___ · ___

Prime factors =
___ · ___ · ___ · ___

Complete a factor tree for each problem.

13. 126	**15.** 46	**17.** 144	**19.** 84
14. 430	**16.** 248	**18.** 137	**20.** 91

EXERCISE 3.2

Arrange the answers in Exercise 3.1 as the products of prime factors. The first problem is done. Beware of several duplications.

1. $81 = 3 \cdot 3 \cdot 3 \cdot 3$	**6.** 21	**11.** 225	**16.** 84
2. 48	**7.** 35	**12.** 48	**17.** 430
3. 225	**8.** 39	**13.** 126	**18.** 248
4. 64	**9.** 90	**14.** 46	**19.** 137
5. 14	**10.** 88	**15.** 144	**20.** 91

CHAPTER 4

Greatest Common Factor

The **greatest common factor** (GCF) of two, or more, numbers is the greatest (largest) number that is a factor of each.

Here are two methods to find the greatest common factor:

Method 1: Listing Factors

> *Find the GCF of 12 and 18.*
>> *Step 1:   List all factors of each number.*
>>
>> *Factors of 12: 1, 2, 3, 4, 6, 12*
>>
>> *Factors of 18: 1, 2, 3, 6, 9, 18*
>>
>> *Step 2:   List all factors in common.*
>>
>> *1, 2, 3, 6*
>>
>> *Step 3:   The largest common factor will be the GCF.*
>>
>> *GCF = 6*

Method 1 is a listing of factors. It is useful for smaller numbers, but becomes cumbersome with larger numbers and multiple numbers.

Method 2: Identifying Common Prime Factors

> *Find the GCF of 60, 30, 90.*
>> *Step 1:   Reduce each number to prime factors using prime factorization.*
>>
>> $30 = 3 \cdot 10 = 3 \cdot 2 \cdot 5$
>>
>> $60 = 6 \cdot 10 = 3 \cdot 2 \cdot 2 \cdot 5$
>>
>> $90 = 3 \cdot 30 = 3 \cdot 3 \cdot 10 = 3 \cdot 3 \cdot 2 \cdot 5$
>>
>> *This form is a variation of the factor tree.*
>>
>> *Step 2:   List all prime factors the numbers have in common.*
>>
>> *2, 3, 5*
>>
>> *Step 3:   Multiply the common prime numbers together to get the GCF.*
>>
>> $2 \cdot 3 \cdot 5 = 30$
>>
>> *GCF = 30*

Method 2 breaks factors into only prime numbers (prime factors). The common prime factors when identified and then multiplied together give the GCF.

Using Method Two, suppose composite numbers have *multiples* of the same factor in common. Common multiple factors are multiplied together in determining the GCF.

Example

$12 = 2 \cdot 2 \cdot 3$ *12 contains two factors of 2 in common with 16*

$16 = 2 \cdot 2 \cdot 2 \cdot 2$ *16 contains two factors of 2 in common with 12*

The GCF of 12 and 16 is the product of 2 · 2. GCF = 4.

EXERCISE 4.1

What is the GCF for each pair of numbers?

1. $6 = 2 \cdot 3$
   $4 = 2 \cdot 2$

2. $36 = 2 \cdot 3 \cdot 2 \cdot 3$
   $45 = 3 \cdot 3 \cdot 5$

3. $100 = 2 \cdot 2 \cdot 5 \cdot 5$
   $25 = 5 \cdot 5$

4. $8 = 2 \cdot 2 \cdot 2$
   $12 = 2 \cdot 2 \cdot 3$

5. $18 = 3 \cdot 3 \cdot 2$
   $42 = 3 \cdot 7 \cdot 2$

6. $56 = 2 \cdot 2 \cdot 2 \cdot 7$
   $84 = 2 \cdot 2 \cdot 3 \cdot 7$

7. $24 = 2 \cdot 2 \cdot 2 \cdot 3$
   $16 = 2 \cdot 2 \cdot 2 \cdot 2$

8. $64 = 2 \cdot 2 \cdot 2 \cdot 2 \cdot 2 \cdot 2$
   $80 = 2 \cdot 2 \cdot 2 \cdot 2 \cdot 5$

9. $28 = 2 \cdot 2 \cdot 7$
   $42 = 2 \cdot 3 \cdot 7$

10. $64 = 2 \cdot 2 \cdot 2 \cdot 2 \cdot 2 \cdot 2$
    $28 = 2 \cdot 2 \cdot 7$

11. $90 = 2 \cdot 3 \cdot 3 \cdot 5$
    $126 = 2 \cdot 3 \cdot 3 \cdot 7$

12. $66 = 2 \cdot 3 \cdot 11$
    $88 = 2 \cdot 2 \cdot 2 \cdot 11$

EXERCISE 4.2

Find the GCF for each set.

1. 3
   7

2. 18
   30

3. 15
   35

4. 6
   36

5. 42
   28

6. 20
   35

7. 24
   40

8. 36
   45

9. 11
   21

10. 60
    36

11. 30
    50

12. 81
    27

13. 54
    66

14. 64
    40

15. 19
    57

16. 6
    8
    4

17. 80
    10
    15

18. 36
    24
    48

19. 12
    27
    42

EXERCISE 4.3

Factor each tree. Determine the GCF for each set. For example:

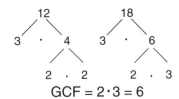

GCF = 2·3 = 6

1.

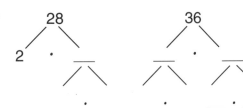

2.

3.

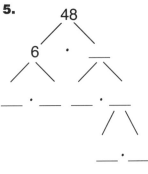

4.

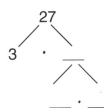

5.

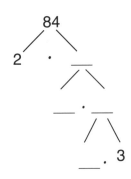

6.

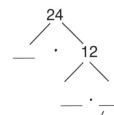

7.

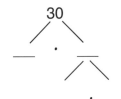

8.

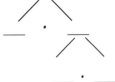

CHAPTER 5

Exponents

An **exponent** is the number of times a base number is used as a factor:

4^2 4 is the **base** number.

^{2} is the **exponent**.

4 is used twice as a factor, $4 \cdot 4$.

The product is the composite number 16.

Exponents are a shorthand to represent repeated multiplication. They are frequently used in scientific notations and algebraic expressions.

The word **power** can be used to refer to exponents. For instance, 4^2 can be referred to as "4 to the power of 2." The power of 2 is often referred to as, in the 4^2 instance, "4 squared. " The "power of 3," as in 4^3, is often referred to as "4 cubed."

Other examples of exponents are:

$7 = 7$ to the power of 1.

$3^2 = 3$ to the second power, or $3 \cdot 3 = 9$.

$5^3 = 5$ to the third power, or $5 \cdot 5 \cdot 5 = 125$.

$2^4 = 2$ to the fourth power, or $2 \cdot 2 \cdot 2 \cdot 2 = 16$.

EXERCISE 5.1

Write each of the following as an exponent.

1. 9 to the seventh power

2. 3 squared

3. $4 \cdot 4 \cdot 4$

4. 8

5. $132 \cdot 132$

6. 17 to the fifth power

7. $10 \cdot 10$

8. $8 \cdot 8 \cdot 8 \cdot 8 \cdot 8$

9. $15 \cdot 15 \cdot 15 \cdot 15$

10. $2 \cdot 2 \cdot 2 \cdot 2 \cdot 2 \cdot 2$

11. 7 cubed

12. 9 to the fourth power

EXERCISE 5.2

Find the value of each expression.

1. 3^2
2. 2^5
3. 3^3
4. 4^2
5. 1^{10}

6. 7^2
7. 5^3
8. 2^4
9. 4^4
10. 10^2

11. 9^3
12. 11^2
13. 6^4
14. 30^3
15. 15^1

EXERCISE 5.3

Rewrite each of the following expressions as an exponent with a base number of 2, 3, 5, 7, or 10.

1. 25
2. 81
3. 10,000

4. 64
5. 343
6. 3125

7. 10,000,000
8. 625
9. 256

CHAPTER 6

Least Common Multiple

The **Least Common Multiple** (LCM) of two, or more, numbers is the least (smallest) number that is a factor of each, except zero. It is the first number into which each can divide evenly.

There are two methods to find the LCM:

Method 1: Listing Multiples

Find the LCM of 3 and 5.
Step 1: List the multiples of each number.
Multiples of 3 = 0, 3, 6, 9, 12, 15, 18....
Multiples of 5 = 0, 5, 10, 15, 20, 25....
Step 2: Identify the first number that each has in common.
3 = 0, 3, 6, 9, 12, **15**, 18....
5 = 0, 5, 10, **15**, 20, 25....
LCM = 15

Method 2: Listing Prime Factors

Find the LCM of 18, 27, and 30.
Step 1: Reduce each number to its prime factors.
$18 = 2 \cdot 3 \cdot 3$
$27 = 3 \cdot 3 \cdot 3$
$30 = 2 \cdot 3 \cdot 5$
Step 2: Express prime factors as exponents.
$18 = 2 \cdot 3 \cdot 3 = 2 \cdot 3^2$
$27 = 3 \cdot 3 \cdot 3 = 3^3$
$30 = 2 \cdot 3 \cdot 5 = 2 \cdot 3 \cdot 5$

Step 3: Select the highest exponent for each prime number and find their product.

$18 = 2 \cdot 3 \cdot 3 = \mathbf{2} \cdot 3^2$

$27 = 3 \cdot 3 \cdot 3 = \mathbf{3^3}$

$30 = 2 \cdot 3 \cdot 5 = 2 \cdot 3 \cdot \mathbf{5}$

$LCM = 2 \cdot 3^3 \cdot 5$

$LCM = 2 \cdot 27 \cdot 5$

$LCM = 270$

Method 2 requires that you sift through all prime factors and select the prime factors with their highest exponents. Multiplication follows.

Take the prime factor 3 as it is gained from 18, 27, and 30. 3 has exponents of 3^1, 3^2, and 3^3. Only the highest exponent (power) 3^3 is selected and then multiplied by the highest exponent of 2 (2^1) and the highest exponent of 5 (5^1): $2 \cdot 3^3 \cdot 5 = 270$.

EXERCISE 6.1

Find the LCM for each set of numbers.

1. 4, 6	**6.** 2, 10	**11.** 12, 32
2. 12, 16	**7.** 10, 15	**12.** 18, 24
3. 5, 6	**8.** 7, 6	**13.** 27, 36
4. 6, 8	**9.** 15, 35	**14.** 21, 48
5. 4, 9	**10.** 8, 20	**15.** 24, 56

EXERCISE 6.2

Find the LCM for each set of numbers.

1. 8, 9	**5.** 6, 8, 12	**9.** 8, 10, 25
2. 15, 75	**6.** 7, 21, 84	**10.** 12, 16, 24
3. 14, 21	**7.** 9, 12, 15	**11.** 14, 18, 21
4. 3, 4, 6	**8.** 6, 9, 15	**12.** 20, 36, 48

EXERCISE 6.3

Find the GCF and the LCM.

1. 21, 36	**5.** 15, 36, 75
2. 18, 24	**6.** 6, 60, 100
3. 6, 9, 12	**7.** 6, 9, 18
4. 9, 21, 36	**8.** 14, 42, 49

CHAPTER 7

Variables

A **variable** is a symbol (e.g.: x, Δ, Σ) used to represent a missing number.

A variable is often used with a number (coefficient) and within a mathematical statement (formula).

Examples

$12y$	*The **coefficient** 12 and the **variable** y form the **term** 12y.*
$x = 6 + 3$	*A formula stating that the variable x is equal to 9.*

If, as in the first example, the variable y is known to be 4, the term $12y$ can be evaluated by substituting 4 for y.

$12y = 12(4)$ Substitution of 4 for y.
$12y = 48$ Evaluation.

If, as in the second example, a formula ($x = 6 + 3$) contains a variable, the variable (x) can be determined by completing the operation of addition:

$x = 6 + 3$ The operation of addition establishes what the
$x = 9$ variable x equals.

EXERCISE 7.1

Evaluate these expressions using these values: a = 8; b = 5; c = 3; d = 9.

1. $a + 13$
2. $27 - d$
3. $19 + b$
4. $d - 2$
5. $c + 15$

6. $152 - d$
7. $a + 21 + b$
8. $30 - d - c$
9. $a + b - 7$
10. $d + a + b$

11. $72 - a - 17$
12. $42 + 10 - d$
13. $a + 12 - b$
14. $b + c - a$
15. $b + d + 52$

EXERCISE 7.2

Solve for the variable in each equation.

1. $x = 24 - 6$
2. $a = 15 + 8$
3. $35 - 24 = d$
4. $42 + 17 = m$
5. $h = 12 \cdot 6$
6. $y = 325 + 14$

7. $s = 1400 - 687$
8. $g = 1542 + 1092$
9. $227 - 143 = w$
10. $827 + 119 = k$
11. $3(12) = v$
12. $587 + 263 = h$

13. $k = 26 + 327$
14. $z = 127 - 98$
15. $42 + 1971 = c$
16. $z = 15 \cdot 15$
17. $268 + 268 = y$
18. $t = 2001 - 1003$

Organizing Variables

Variables can be gathered together by collecting like terms. **Like terms** are terms that contain the same variables. Terms with variables are ordered alphabetically.

Examples

$5x + 6x + 3y =$
$\mathbf{5x} + 6y + \mathbf{3x} = \mathbf{8x} + 6y$ *Collect the like terms $5x$ and $3x$ to equal $8x$.*

$12b - 6c - 5b =$
$\mathbf{12b} - 6c - \mathbf{5b} = \mathbf{7b} - 6c$ *Collect the like terms $12b$ and $-5b$ to equal $7b$.*

$5 + y =$
$5 + y = 5 + y$ *There are no like terms to collect.*

EXERCISE 7.3

Collect like terms.

1. $12m + 7m$ 19m
2. $237x - 137x$
3. $52a + 17c - 12c$
4. $7w + 8x + 12y$
5. $23d + 4g - 12d$

6. $a + b + c + 3a - b$
7. $24 + 9z - 24$
8. $32c - 17d - 6 + 21d$
9. $2e + 4f - 9g - e$
10. $24 - 27a - 15 + 82a$

11. $7m - 4n + 6 - 2m$
12. $15r + 16s - 12r - 12s - 17$
13. $d - c + 2 + 12d - 1$
14. $2x + 2xy + 3c - xy$
15. $12ab - a + 2bc - 3ab - bc$

Operations with a Combination of Whole Numbers and Variables

You have been introduced to operations with simple addition, subtraction, and multiplication of variables. Now, division will be added as well as operations that include a combination of whole numbers and variables.

• **Addition of variables**

Examples

Adding similiar variables

$2x + 3x = 5x$ *Collect x terms.*

$15a + 17b + a = 16a + 17b$ *Collect like terms and order alphabetically.*

Adding whole numbers and variables

$24 + 24a + 21 = 24a + 45$ *Collect like terms and whole numbers.*

$7y + 10 + 9b + 15 = 9b + 7y + 25$ *Collect like terms, order alphabetically, whole numbers last.*

• **Subtraction of variables**

Examples

Subtracting similiar variables

$25g - 7g = 18g$ *Collect g terms.*

$35c - 10d - c = 34c - 10d$ *Collect and order terms.*

Subtracting whole numbers and variables

$42m - 29 - 15m = 27m - 29$ *Collect and order terms.*

$6c - 5d - 10 - 4c = 2c - 5d - 10$ *Collect and order terms.*

• **Multiplication of variables**

Examples

Multiplying two variables

$m \cdot n = mn$

$s \cdot s = s^2$

Multiplying whole numbers and variables

$10 \cdot c = 10c$

$4 \cdot x = 4x$

Multiplying whole numbers and terms containing a variable

$7 \cdot 5d = 35d$ Step 1: Multiply $7 \cdot 5$

Step 2: Place the variable (d) after the product of $7 \cdot 5$

$15r \cdot 3 = 45r$ Step 1: Multiply $15 \cdot 3$

Step 2: Place the variable (r) after the product of $15 \cdot 3$

Multiplying two expressions each containing a variable

$9c \cdot 7d = 63cd$ Step 1: Multiply the coefficients: $9 \cdot 7$

Step 2: Multiply the variables $c \cdot d$

$8g \cdot 4g = 32g^2$ Step 1: Multiply the coefficients: $8 \cdot 4$

Step 2: Multiply the variables $g \cdot g$

EXERCISE 7.4

Combine these variables.

1. $a \cdot b$		**7.** $3y \cdot 4z$		**13.** $cd \cdot g$	
2. $15c \cdot 5$		**8.** $124 \cdot 2h$		**14.** $2c \cdot c \cdot 4$	
3. $10x \cdot 12x$		**9.** $15 \cdot 15$		**15.** $7 \cdot 6b \cdot 2$	
4. $4d \cdot 23$		**10.** $11k \cdot 15j$		**16.** $w \cdot w \cdot w$	
5. $m \cdot m$		**11.** $2v \cdot v$		**17.** $3a \cdot 3b \cdot 3c$	
6. $12r \cdot 12s$		**12.** $130s \cdot t$		**18.** $8m^2 \cdot 5m$	

• **Division of variables and numbers**

Examples

Dividing like variables

$w \div w = 1$

$x^2 \div x = x$

Dividing with different variables

$c \div d = \frac{c}{d}$

Dividing with coefficients and variables

$12v \div 3v = 4$ Step 1: Divide the coefficients: $12 \div 3$

Step 2: Divide v by v. They cancel each other: $\frac{12\cancel{v}}{3\cancel{v}} = 4$

Dividing terms with different variables

$14a \div 2b = 7\frac{a}{b}$ Step 1: Divide the coefficients: $14 \div 2$

     Step 2: Divide a by b

$72m \div 9n = 8\frac{m}{n}$ Step 1: Divide coefficients: $72 \div 9$

     Step 2: Divide m by n

$60xy \div 12x = 5y$ Step 1: Divide coefficients: $60 \div 5$

     Step 2: Divide xy by x: $\frac{x\!\!\!/y}{x\!\!\!/} = y$

EXERCISE 7.5

Perform the operation of division.

1. $c \div c$
2. $2d^2 \div d$
3. $g \div h$
4. $39s \div 13s$
5. $18a \div 6$

6. $24m \div 3n$
7. $375x \div 15y$
8. $45ab \div 3a$
9. $60a^2b \div 12a$
10. $uv \div u$

11. $a^3 \div a$
12. $27z \div 9p$
13. $2w \div 2w$
14. $12b \div b$
15. $81mn^2 \div 9m$

EXERCISE 7.6

Review. Perform all operations possible. Order answers properly.

1. $12b + 3a - 7b$
2. $\frac{39m}{13m}$
3. $15c - 3c - 11c$
4. $t \cdot u \cdot v$
5. $42 \cdot n$
6. $3c - 7d$
7. $z \div z$
8. $\frac{ab}{bc}$

9. $32x - 16x + 7xy$
10. $100 - 73 + a + 10a$
11. $12 + 24d + 6c - 5d$
12. $12 \cdot 3c$
13. $\frac{15k}{75m}$
14. $35 - 10 + 7c + 8a$
15. $7r \cdot 8st$
16. $49ef \div 7f$

17. $9s \cdot 9s + 5s$
18. $15c \cdot 15c^2$
19. $6 \cdot 6 \cdot 6d$
20. $w^2 \div vw$
21. $40w \cdot 4w$
22. $\frac{12cd}{36bc}$
23. $126y \div 3y^2$
24. $4g \cdot 4h \cdot 4g$

CHAPTER 8

Properties

Real numbers have properties. That is, they have qualities and relationships that help us understand them better. You have used many of these properites without formally being introduced to them. The purpose of this chapter is to introduce you formally to three properties: the **commutative** property, the **associative** property, and the **distributive** property.

Commutative Property

The **order** in which numbers are added or multiplied does not change their results.

Examples

Addition

$a + b = b + a$ *Variable form.*
$2 + 3 = 3 + 2$ *Let $a = 2$ and $b = 3$.*
$5 = 5$ *The order in adding 2 and 3 does not change the answer, 5.*

Multiplication

$a \cdot b = b \cdot a$ *Variable Form.*
$2 \cdot 3 = 3 \cdot 2$ *Let $a = 2$ and $b = 3$.*
$6 = 6$ *The order in multiplying 2 and 3 does not change the answer, 6.*

EXERCISE 8.1

Reorder these problems using the commutative property.

1. $15 + 6 + x =$ 4. $3 \cdot 5 \cdot 7 \cdot 8 =$ 7. $10w \cdot 35x =$

2. $a \cdot 5c =$ 5. $3 \cdot 4 \cdot 5 =$ 8. $a + b =$

3. $6 + 8 + 4 =$ 6. $17 + y =$ 9. $13 + 9 + 1 =$

EXERCISE 8.2

Explain why this problem does not demonstrate the commutative property.

1. $2 \div 1 = 2$

Associative Property

The **grouping** in which numbers are added or multiplied does not change their result.

Example

Addition

$(a + b) + c = a + (b + c)$ *Variable form.*

$(2 + 3) + 4 = 2 + (3 + 4)$ *Let a = 2, b = 3, and c = 4.*

$5 + 4 = 2 + 7$ *The grouping by parentheses does not change*

$9 = 9$ *the answer, 9.*

Multiplication

$(a \cdot b) \cdot c = a \cdot (b \cdot c)$ *Variable form.*

$(2 \cdot 3) \cdot 4 = 2 \cdot (3 \cdot 4)$ *The grouping by parentheses does not change*

$6 \cdot 4 = 2 \cdot 12$ *the answer, 24.*

$24 = 24$

EXERCISE 8.3

Regroup these problems using their associative properties.

1. $(78 + 4) + 7 =$ **4.** $(27 \cdot 5) \cdot 7 =$ **7.** $5 + (7 + 6) + 4 =$

2. $3 \cdot (7 \cdot 2) =$ **5.** $15 + (25 + 17) =$ **8.** $7 \cdot 5 \cdot (8 \cdot 6) =$

3. $(32 + 6) + 9 =$ **6.** $10 \cdot (19 \cdot 5) =$ **9.** $(12 + 15) + 16 =$

EXERCISE 8.4

Explain why this problem does not demonstrate the associative property.

1. $(24 \div 6) \div 2 = 2$

The commutative property reorders and the associative property regroups. Regrouping is usually done by the placement of parentheses, which may be a tip-off to the use of the associative property. But, what about this problem? Does it illustrate the commutative or the associative property?

$$3 + (6 + 4) = 3 + (4 + 6)$$

The commutative property of addition. In this example, a grouping has been reordered. Here is the same idea with the commutative property of multiplication:

$$5(11 \cdot 9) = 5(9 \cdot 11)$$

Distributive Property

The distributive property will take greater explanation. It is most often used to show a relationship between mutiplication and addition–although, subtraction can be distributed in some instances.

When multiplication and addition are involved, the relationship is formally called the distributive property of multiplication over addition. When the sum of two numbers is to be multiplied by another number, the other number can be used (distributed) with each of the numbers to be added, multiplying each one separately.

Example

$$a \cdot (b + c) = a \cdot b + a \cdot c$$ *Variable form. Let a = 2, b = 3, and c = 4.*

$$2 \cdot (3 + 4) = 2 \cdot 3 + 2 \cdot 4$$ *The 2 is distributed to the 3 and 4.*

$$2 \cdot 7 = 6 + 8$$

$$14 = 14$$ *The distribution does not change the answer.*

EXERCISE 8.5

Show how these expressions can be distributed.

1. $4(4 + 7) =$
2. $12(60 + 5) =$
3. $8(12 - 6) =$
4. $9(6 - 4) =$
5. $4(6 + 5 - 3) =$
6. $10(14 + 10) =$

EXERCISE 8.6

Work each problem in 8.5 through to prove the distribution property.

EXERCISE 8.7

State the single property illustrated in each problem: commutative, associative, or distributive.

1. $12 \cdot 4 \cdot 3 = 3 \cdot 4 \cdot 12$
2. $2(3 + 6) = (2 \cdot 3) + (2 \cdot 6)$
3. $7(5 - 2) = 7 \cdot 5 - 7 \cdot 2$
4. $(3 \cdot 4)8 = 3(4 \cdot 8)$
5. $24(6) = 6 \cdot 24$
6. $(2 + 3) + 5 = (3 + 2) + 5$
7. $12(14 + 3) = 12(14) + 12(3)$
8. $(8 + 3) + 13 = 8 + (3 + 13)$
9. $5(4 + 3) + 4 = (5 \cdot 4) + (5 \cdot 3) + 4$
10. $7 + (15 + 4) + 7 = 7 + (4 + 15) + 7$
11. $3 + (2 + 5) = (3 + 2) + 5$
12. $5(11 \cdot 6) = (11 \cdot 6)5$

EXERCISE 8.8

What two properties are at work here?

1. $(3 \cdot 9)2 = 3(2 \cdot 9)$

CHAPTER 9

Integers

This chapter introduces you to **integers** that are whole numbers, their opposites, and zero: 12, –12, 0. In a later chapter, you will be introduced to integers in rational (fractional) form.

Integers help in comparing directions that agree with certain events. Integers, because they include the use of positive and negative signs, are sometimes referred to as **signed numbers**: +12, –12. You will learn to compare and order integers while performing basic operations (+, –, x, ÷) with them.

Let's begin simply. Using a plus or minus sign and a whole number, (together a formal integer), how would you represent: 20° below zero?

$$20° \text{ below zero} = –20°$$

EXERCISE 9.1

Provide an integer to represent each description. Remember to use a + or – sign.

1. An altitude of 7200 feet
2. A loss of 15 pounds
3. A pay raise of $1500
4. A withdrawal of $124 from an ATM
5. Two hundred feet below sea level

6. An investment loss of $27,000
7. The opposite of –57
8. A weight gain of 34 pounds
9. A 15 yard gain in football
10. The opposite of 9

This is a **number line** where we will use only whole numbers to represent and compare integers:

-10 -9 -8 -7 -6 -5 -4 -3 -2 -1 **0** 1 2 3 4 5 6 7 8 9 10
Negative Numbers   *Positive Numbers*

EXERCISE 9.2

Use the number line as a guide to answer these twelve questions.

1. What number is 5 units to the right of –4?
2. What number is 3 units to the left of 2?
3. What number is 9 units right of –10?

4. What number is 4 units right of 3?
5. What number is 7 units left of seven?
6. What number is 6 units less than 5?

Exercise 9.2, con't.

7. Begin with +5: move +2, move –3. Answer =

8. Begin with 0: move +6, move –9. Answer =

9. Begin with –7: move –4, move –11. Answer =

10. 10: move –4, move +11. Answer =

11. 3: move –4, move –3, move +12. Answer =

12. –7: +9, –3. Answer =

Addition of Integers

• **Addition of integers with the same sign.**

If all numbers are positive, add the numerals.

If all numbers are negative, add the numerals and place negative sign in front of the result.

Examples

$6 + 4 = c$ *Both 6 and 4 are postive numbers.*

$10 = c$ *Add both numerals. 10 is understood as +10.*

$-6 + -4 = c$ *Both –6 and –4 are negative numbers.*

$-10 = c$ *Add both numbers, place a negative sign in front of the result.*

EXERCISE 9.3

Find the sum.

1. $7 + 2$

2. $-3 + -6$

3. $8 + 14$

4. $-5 + -2$

5. $-52 + -1$

6. $-1 + -52$

7. $47 + 16$

8. $7 + 8 + 9$

9. $-7 + -8 + -9$

10. $-17 + -11 + -6$

11. $12 + 6 + 18$

12. $-8 + -2 + -10$

EXERCISE 9.4

Solve these problems

1. $b = -6 + -6$

2. $d = -9 + -5$

3. $8 + 4 = a$

4. $g = -32 + -75$

5. $-6 + -9 + -12 = m$

6. $s = -23 + -37 + -42$

7. $-152 + -421 = w$

8. $52 + 17 + 91 = x$

9. $-5 + -24 + -12 = z$

• Addition of integers with the different signs.

If only one number is negative, subtract the smaller numeral from the larger numeral. Place a negative sign before the result **only** if the larger numeral was negative.

Examples

8 + –2 6	*One number is negative. Subtract the smaller number from the larger. Subtract 2 from 8. The result is positive: 8 is larger than 2.*
2 + –8 –6	*One number is negative. Subtract the smaller number from the larger. Subtract 2 from 8. The result is negative: 8 was larger **and** a negative number.*

EXERCISE 9.5

Find the sum.

1. –4 + 3
2. 6 + –9
3. 7 + –10
4. –6 + 5

5. 15 + –24
6. –47 + 30
7. –19 + 12
8. 23 + –52

9. –147 + 88
10. 232 + –329
11. 162 + –180
12. –141 + 7

EXERCISE 9.6

Solve these problems.

1. n = –5 + 4
2. 3 + –12 = a
3. –54 + 28 = b

4. 94 + –19 = x
5. d = –52 + 67
6. p = 54 + –88

7. r = –38 + 19
8. w = 39 + –42
9. 41 + –43 = z

EXERCISE 9.7

Solve these problems.

1. d = –17 + 32
2. c = –28 + –17
3. –127 + 58 = b
4. 72 + 89 = r
5. –42 + –77 = w

6. 32 + –17 = a
7. g = 427 + –92
8. m = –238 + 176
9. p = 13 + –27
10. 35 + 79 = y

11. 127 + –692 = k
12. –63 + –39 = c
13. a = 32 + 17
14. e = –38 + 128
15. x = 26 + – 129

Subtraction of integers.

To subtract integers, replace the subtraction symbol with the addition symbol. Change the second number to its opposite. Follow the rules for addition of integers.

Examples

$8 - 10$	*Replace the – symbol with the + symbol. Change 10 to –10.*
$8 + (-10)$	*Follow the rules for addition of integers with different signs.*
-2	
$15 - 12 = y$	*Replace the – symbol with the + symbol. Change 12 to –12.*
$15 + (-12) = y$	*Follow the rules for addition of integers with different signs.*
$3 = y$	
$-6 - (-10)$	*Replace the – symbol with the + symbol. Change –10 to 10.*
$-6 + 10$	*Follow the rules for addition of integers with different signs.*
4	
$z = 16 - (-15)$	*Replace the – symbol with the + symbol. Change –15 to 15.*
$z = 16 + 15$	*Follow the rules for addition of integers with the same signs.*
$z = 31$	

EXERCISE 9.8

Without solving each problem, state whether each answer will be – or +.

1. $23 - 30$
2. $29 - 18$
3. $-6 - -10$
4. $6 - 10$
5. $-12 - (-19)$
6. $12 - -8$

7. $-15 - -14$
8. $-25 - (-19)$
9. $0 - -15$
10. $-37 - 37$
11. $60 - (-83)$
12. $-125 - 153$

13. $-270 - (-127)$
14. $270 - -127$
15. $-127 - 127$
16. $270 - 127$
17. $321 - (-12)$
18. $-21 - 72$

EXERCISE 9.9

Solve each problem in Exercise 9.8.

EXERCISE 9.10

Solve each equation.

1. $q = -4 - -3$
2. $-7 - (-8) = a$
3. $b = 8 - 14$
4. $9 - 31 = k$

5. $p = 23 - 37$
6. $r = -27 - (-15)$
7. $s = 62 - 37$
8. $-45 - 39 = t$

9. $x = -48 - (-26)$
10. $y = 58 - 85$
11. $z = -125 - 510$
12. $-472 - 700 = a$

Multiplication of integers.

If the signs (– or +) are the same, the answer is positive. If the signs are different, the answer is negative.

Examples

$-8 \cdot 7$	*Signs are different.*
-56	*Answer is negative.*
$a = -9(-12)$	*Signs are the same.*
$a = 108$	*Answer is positive.*
$8 \cdot 9$	*Signs are the same.*
72	*Answer is positive.*

EXERCISE 9.11

State the sign for each product.

1. $-4(6)$
2. $4 \cdot 25$
3. $9 \cdot -12$
4. $-6(-9)$
5. $-12 \cdot -30$

6. $(-37)\,(-15)$
7. $-4 \cdot 82$
8. $428 \cdot -17$
9. $-24 \cdot -17$
10. $15(32)$

11. $(-18)\,(-18)$
12. 18^2
13. $33 \cdot -33$
14. $-9(-14)$
15. $(21)\,(15)$

EXERCISE 9.12

Solve each problem in Exercise 9.11.

EXERCISE 9.13

Solve each problem.

1. $b = -7(24)$
2. $-4 \cdot -15 = a$
3. $c = 8 \cdot -17$
4. $-12 \cdot -15 = d$
5. $(25)\,(-5) = g$

6. $-5(24) = h$
7. $k = (40)\,(9)$
8. $m = (-3)\,(27)$
9. $n = 8(-12)$
10. $-19 \cdot 4 = p$

11. $r = 12^2$
12. $s = -6(36)$
13. $12 \cdot -12 - t$
14. $w = -5 \cdot -14$
15. $x = -11(15)$

Division of integers.

Division follows multiplication in determining signs. If signs are the same, the answer is positive. If the signs are different, the answer is negative.

Division can be presented in two forms:

$$\text{FORM 1: } 15 \div -3 \qquad \text{and} \qquad \text{FORM 2: } \frac{15}{-3}$$

Form 1 involves ordinary numbers used as integers. Form 2 involves a rational number composed of integers. (More about rational numbers and integers in Chapter 11.)

In the Form 1 model ($15 \div -3$), different signs give a negative answer. In Form 2 model ($\frac{15}{-3}$), the numerator is positive and the denominator is negative: different signs give a negative answer. Both forms have an answer of –5.

Examples

$\frac{-36}{12} = -3$ *Sign of the numerator is different from the denominator. Answer is negative.*

$-36 \div 12 = -3$ *Signs are different. Answer is negative.*

$a = \frac{75}{-5} = -15$ *Sign of the numerator is different from the denominator. Answer is negative.*

$\frac{-3}{-6} = \frac{1}{2}$ *Same signs. Positive answer.*

EXERCISE 9.14

State the sign for each answer.

1.	$18 \div 2$	**6.**	$-48 \div -16$	**11.**	$-4 \div -8$
2.	$-18 \div 2$	**7.**	$72 \div 12$	**12.**	$-\frac{105}{5}$
3.	$\frac{15}{-3}$	**8.**	$99 \div -33$	**13.**	$-18 \div 3$
4.	$\frac{-15}{3}$	**9.**	$\frac{7}{21}$	**14.**	$\frac{49}{-14}$
5.	$-\frac{15}{3}$	**10.**	$51 \div 17$	**15.**	$\frac{-5}{25}$

EXERCISE 9.15

Solve each problem in Exercise 9.14.

EXERCISE 9.16

Solve each problem.

1. $48 \div 4$
2. $-32 \div 8$
3. $21 \div -3$
4. $-80 \div -16$
5. $-72 \div 9$

6. $81 \div 9$
7. $108 \div 12$
8. $-54 \div -4$
9. $-64 \div 16$
10. $-320 \div -10$

11. $121 \div -11$
12. $-105 \div 5$
13. $-36 \div 6$
14. $-15 \div -15$
15. $175 \div 50$

EXERCISE 9.17

Solve each problem.

1. $a = \frac{250}{-25}$
2. $-\frac{120}{15} = y$
3. $\frac{-75}{15} = z$

4. $a = \frac{-144}{-3}$
5. $b = \frac{98}{-7}$
6. $\frac{-143}{11} = c$

7. $\frac{-343}{7} = w$
8. $-\frac{804}{67} = n$
9. $\frac{-12}{-48} = s$

Extending Operations with Integers

How do you handle signs when more than two numbers are involved or when several operations are involved? So far, rules have been given for single operations (addition, subtraction, multiplication, or division) involving only two sign numbers.

For multiple numbers with signs, here are the procedures: an even number of negative signs gives a positive answer; an odd number of negative signs gives a negative answer; no negative signs gives a positive answer.

Examples

$(-2) (-3) (4)$ *You know in advance: an even number of negative signs = + answer.*
       $6(4)$ $-2 \cdot -3 = (positive)\ 6$
         24 $6 \cdot 4 = 24$

$-10 \div 5(-3) (-2)$ *An odd number of negative signs = – answer.*
    $-2(-3) (-2)$ *Work left to right (Order of Operations): $-10 \div 5 = -2$.*
        $6(-2)$ $-2 \cdot -3 = 6.$
          -12 $6 \cdot -2 = -12.$

EXERCISE 9.18

Solve these problems. Remember the Order of Operations.

1. (–1) (3) (–3)

2. (–6) (–2) (–5)

3. 56 ÷ –7 · 5

4. –12 ÷ (–6) (7) ÷ –2

5. 88 ÷ 11(6) (–4)

6. (–3) (–2) (–6) (–5)

7. –12 ÷ 2 ÷ –6

8. –6(–3) ÷ 6 · 2

9. –20 ÷ 4(–4)

10. (–24) ÷ –6 ÷ 2

11. 5(–6) ÷ 15(–5)

12. –135 ÷ –15(–9) ÷ 9

Order of Operations Revisited.

Let's incorporate all that has been presented about integers and sign numbers with your knowledge of the Order of Operations. Here are the orderly procedures to keep in mind:

1. Solve operations within parentheses and remove parentheses.

2. Calculate any exponents.

3. Solve multiplication or division from left to right.

4. Solve addition or subtraction from left to right.

Examples

$-3(5 - 2) \div 3 \, (4 \cdot 5)$ *Work within parentheses: subtract, and multiply.*

$-3(3) \div 3(20)$ *Remove parentheses.*

$-9 \div 3 \cdot 20$ *Work from left to right: divide.*

$-3 \cdot 20$ *Then, multiply.*

-60

From the beginning, there is an odd number of negative signed numbers. Don't be confused with $(5 - 2)$*. This negative sign is for the operation of subtraction; 2 by itself is a positive integer.*

$b = \dfrac{(5 \, \cdot \, -8)(-2 \, \cdot \, -4)}{10} \div - 2$ *Work within parentheses: multiply.*

$= \dfrac{(-40) \cdot (8)}{10} \div - 2$ *Remove parentheses: multiply.*

$= \dfrac{-320}{10} \div - 2$ *Work from left to right: divide.*

$= - 32 \div - 2$ *Divide again.*

$= 16$

EXERCISE 9.19

Remembering the Order of Operations, solve these problems.

1. $13 + -51 \div 3$

2. $\dfrac{(13 + -52)}{3}$

3. $5(-6 + 2)$

4. $(16 + -9) + (4 \div 2)$

5. $(5 \cdot 6)(-12 \div -6)$

6. $16 \div 4 + 12 \cdot 3 + -6$

7. $-18 \div (-3) + 5(-7)$

8. $-14 + (6 \cdot 4) \div 2$

9. $(50 + 36)(-2 \div -2)$

10. $-36 \div (-9) - 4(2)$

11. $\dfrac{(-4 + 6)(-2)}{(5)(-3) - (-3)}$

12. $24 \div 8 \cdot 3(-1)$

13. $9(-2)(6) \div 3(-3) + 5$

14. $\dfrac{3(4 - 2)}{2(4 + 3) - 4}$

15. $28 \div 4 + (3 \cdot -6) - 3(-4 + 2)$

16. $-853 - (-780) + (-350)$

17. $\dfrac{4(-6) - (-3)}{-7 - (-2 - 8)}$

18. $\dfrac{2(6 + -3)(15 \div 3) + 6}{4(5 + 3) - 2(21 \div 3)}$

CHAPTER 10

More with Exponents

You already know that in the expression 5^4, 5 is the base and ^{4} is the exponent. 5^4 is read as "5 raised to the 4th power." 5 has 4 factors of 5 ($5 \cdot 5 \cdot 5 \cdot 5$) and can be evaluated as 625.

The Invisible One Exponent

If no exponent is shown, the exponent is assumed to be 1.

Examples

$5 = 5^1$ *$5^1 = 5$, or 5 to the 1st power.*

$x = x^1$ *$x^1 = x$, or x to the 1st power.*

$y = y^1$ *$y^1 = y$, or y to the 1st power.*

Multiplication

To multiply expressions with the same base, recopy the base and add the exponents.

Examples

$3^2 \cdot 3^3$ *Same base of 3.* $3^2 \cdot 3^3 = 3^{2+3} = 3^5$

$x^5 \cdot x^4$ *Same base of x.* $x^5 \cdot x^4 = x^{5+4} = x^9$

$m^6 \cdot m^7$ *Same base of m.* $m^6 \cdot m^7 = m^{6+7} = m^{13}$

Consider this expression $(4^2)^3$. It is an example of **raising a power (4^2) to another power** $(4^2)^3$. To raise a power to another power, recopy the base and multiply exponents:

Examples

$(4^2)^3$ *Raise 4 to the second power by the power of 3.* $(4^2)^3 = 4^{2 \cdot 3} = 4^6$

$(y^3)^4$ *Raise y to the third power by the power of 4.* $(y^3)^4 = y^{3 \cdot 4} = y^{12}$

$(z^5)^2$ *Raize z to the fifth power by the power of 2* $(z^5)^2 = z^{5 \cdot 2} = z^{10}$

Division

To divide expressions having the same base, recopy the base and subtract the exponents.

Examples

$6^{10} \div 6^4$ $= 6^{10-4}$ $= 6^6$

$\dfrac{x^4}{x^3}$ $= x^{4-3}$ $= x^1 = x$

$y^5 \div y^2$ $= y^{5-2}$ $= y^3$

Exponents with Coefficients

In the expression $8b^4$, 8 is the coefficient, b is the base, and ^{4} is the exponent.

•Adding and Subtracting Exponential Expressions with Coefficients

In adding and subtracting expression with the same base and the same exponent, simply add or subtract the coefficient. You should be familiar with this process as it was introduced in Chapter 7, Variables.

Examples

$4y^2 + 12y^2 = 16y^2$

$15x^3 - 17x^3 = -2x^3$

$3a^2 + b^2 + 6a^2 = 9a^2 + b^2$

•Multiplying and Dividing Exponential Expressions with Coefficients

For multiplication, multiply the coefficients and add the exponents.

For divison, divide the coefficients and subtract the exponents.

Examples

$(4a^2)\,(5a^4)$ $= 4 \cdot 5 \text{ and } a^2 + a^4$ $= 20a^6$

$(.5x^2)\,(2.5x^5)$ $= .5 \cdot 2.5 \text{ and } x^2 + x^5$ $= 1.25x^7$

$10c^4 \div 2c^2$ $= 10 \div 2 \text{ and } c^4 - c^2$ $= 5c^2$

$\dfrac{17b^6}{34b^2}$ $= 17 \div 34 \text{ and } b^6 - b^2$ $= \frac{1}{2}b^4$

EXERCISE 10.1

Simplify each of the following exponential expressions.

1. $c \cdot c^2$

2. $x^2 \cdot x^3 \cdot x$

3. $3^2 \cdot 3 \cdot 5$

4. $7^2 \div 7$

5. $m^4 \div m^2$

6. $15x^3 - 5x^3 + x^3$

7. $rs^3 \div rs^2$

8. $4^3 \cdot 4^4$

9. $4^3 \div 4^3$

10. $2^4 \cdot 2^3 \cdot 10^2 \cdot 10^4$

11. $\dfrac{a^2}{a^2}$

12. $4g^2 \cdot g^3$

13. $x^a \cdot x^b$

14. $(3^2)^4$

15. $4^2 \cdot (4^2)^4$

16. $3a^2 + b + 7a^2$

17. $(z^2)^5$

18. $(x^2)^2 - (y^2)^2$

19. $3x^2 - 10x - 2x$

20. $(6^4)^2 \cdot (6^3)^4$

21. $(3^5)^3 + (3^4)^2$

22. $(4^8)^3 \cdot (4^7)^2$

23. $(3x^2)^2 - (y^2)^2$

24. $(3^2)^3 \cdot 3^4$

EXERCISE 10.2

Simplify each of the following exponential expressions.

1. $(3b)(5b^2)$

2. $24c^3 \div 8c$

3. $\dfrac{4x}{64x}$

4. $(2.4m)(1.4m)$

5. $(2x^2)(3x^2)(5x)^2$

6. $\dfrac{24w^5}{12w^5}$

7. $(5x)(5x)$

8. $3r^4 \div 6r^2$

9. $(4x^2)(2x^3) \div 4x^2$

10. $127s^4 \div s^2$

11. $6h^4 \div 3h^3$

12. $16w^7 \div 4w^2 \cdot 3w^2$

CHAPTER 11

Rational Numbers and Integers

A **rational number** is a number (other than zero) that can be named in a fraction form with a numerator and with a denominator that is an integer.

In this chapter, rational numbers with signs will reinforce skills in reducing fractions and in finding common denominators.

In working with rational numbers, remember three skills presented in earlier chapters. When working with positive and negative signs, recall **integers** from Chapter 9. When reducing rational numbers (fractions), remember the **GCF** from Chapter 4. When finding common denominators, remember the **LCM** from Chapter 6.

Addition of Rational Numbers

If all rational numbers are positive, simply add the rational numbers together.

If all rational numbers are negative, add the rational numbers and place a negative sign at the front of the result.

If one rational number is negative, subtract the smaller rational number from the larger. Place a negative sign before the result **only** if the larger number is negative, otherwise the answer remains positive.

Examples

$b = \frac{3}{16} + \frac{1}{4}$

$b = \frac{3}{16} - \frac{4}{16}$

$b = \frac{7}{16}$

Change to a common denominator. Both rational numbers are positive. Add numerators. Answer remains positive.

$a = -\frac{1}{3} + -\frac{1}{6}$

$a = -\frac{2}{6} + -\frac{1}{6}$

$a = -\frac{3}{6} = -\frac{1}{2}$

Change to a common denominator. Both rational numbers are negative. Add numerators, place a negative sign in front. Reduce.

$c = -\frac{1}{3} + \frac{1}{4}$

$c = -\frac{4}{12} + \frac{3}{12}$

$c = -\frac{1}{12}$

*Change to a common denominator. The rational numbers have different signs. Place a negative sign in front **because** the larger rational number is negative.*

$d = 3\frac{1}{8} + -2\frac{15}{16}$

$d = 3\frac{2}{16} + -2\frac{15}{16}$

$d = \frac{3}{16}$

*Change to a common denominator. The rational numbers have different signs. Subtract the smaller from the larger. Answer remains positive **because** the larger rational number is positive.*

EXERCISE 11.1

State whether answers to the following problems, if evaluated, would be positive (+), negative (–), or zero (0). Do not solve.

1. $\frac{4}{5} + \frac{2}{3}$

2. $\frac{1}{6} + (-\frac{5}{6})$

3. $-\frac{1}{4} + (-\frac{5}{8})$

4. $-\frac{5}{6} + 0$

5. $-\frac{1}{4} + \frac{1}{2}$

6. $-\frac{1}{2} + \frac{1}{4}$

7. $\frac{5}{9} + (-\frac{5}{9})$

8. $2\frac{1}{3} + 3\frac{3}{4}$

9. $-\frac{5}{8} + 2\frac{7}{8}$

10. $-3\frac{1}{3} + -2\frac{2}{3}$

11. $4 + -1\frac{2}{3}$

12. $1\frac{3}{5} + -4\frac{1}{5}$

EXERCISE 11.2

Solve each problem. Write each answer in simplest form.

1. $\frac{1}{2} + \frac{1}{3}$

2. $-\frac{3}{4} + \frac{1}{4}$

3. $-\frac{1}{5} + -\frac{4}{5}$

4. $-\frac{2}{5} + -\frac{3}{10}$

5. $-\frac{7}{10} + \frac{1}{10}$

6. $\frac{1}{3} + -\frac{1}{12}$

7. $-\frac{1}{5} + (-\frac{2}{5})$

8. $\frac{3}{4} + -\frac{7}{8}$

9. $-\frac{1}{2} + \frac{3}{4}$

10. $-\frac{1}{3} + (-\frac{3}{8})$

11. $\frac{5}{12} + (-\frac{5}{8})$

12. $\frac{3}{5} + (-\frac{3}{10})$

EXERCISE 11.3

Solve each problem.

1. $x = -2 + \frac{2}{3}$

2. $y = 6\frac{3}{4} + (-1\frac{1}{2})$

3. $-2\frac{1}{3} + 3\frac{1}{6} = a$

4. $b = 4 + -1\frac{5}{6}$

5. $w = -\frac{5}{6} + (-\frac{3}{8})$

6. $m = -5\frac{5}{6} + (-4\frac{1}{3})$

7. $-4\frac{1}{2} + 2\frac{7}{8} = g$

8. $3\frac{5}{8} + (-\frac{3}{4}) = k$

9. $n = 3\frac{1}{3} + (-2\frac{1}{4})$

10. $-3\frac{1}{4} + (-3\frac{5}{8}) = z$

11. $r = -4 + 1\frac{7}{8}$

12. $q = 7\frac{3}{4} + -4\frac{1}{8}$

Subtraction of Rational Numbers

To subtract a rational number, add its opposite.

Examples

$\frac{1}{5} - (-\frac{3}{5})$

$\frac{1}{5} + \frac{3}{5}$

$\frac{4}{5}$

Subtract $(-\frac{3}{5})$,
adding its opposite, $\frac{3}{5}$

$a = \frac{1}{3} - \frac{3}{4}$

$a = \frac{4}{12} - \frac{9}{12}$

$a = \frac{4}{12} + (-\frac{9}{12})$

$a = -\frac{5}{12}$

Find the LCD. Note: $\frac{9}{12}$ is a positve rational number.
Subtract $\frac{9}{12}$ by adding its opposite, $-\frac{9}{12}$.

$2\frac{1}{2} - 4\frac{5}{12} = x$

$2\frac{6}{12} - 4\frac{5}{12} = x$

$2\frac{6}{12} + (-4\frac{5}{12}) = x$

$1\frac{11}{12} = x$

Find the LCD. Note: $4\frac{5}{12}$ is a positive rational number.
Subtract $4\frac{5}{12}$ by adding its opposite, $-4\frac{5}{12}$.

EXERCISE 11.4

Change each subtraction problem to an addition problem.

1. $\frac{2}{3} - \frac{1}{3}$

2. $-\frac{1}{8} - (-\frac{3}{4})$

3. $\frac{1}{2} - \frac{1}{4}$

4. $\frac{1}{3} - (-\frac{5}{6})$

5. $5 - (-\frac{5}{12})$

6. $4\frac{1}{4} - 5$

7. $-2\frac{1}{4} - 3\frac{3}{4}$

8. $4\frac{1}{2} - 6\frac{1}{2}$

9. $-1\frac{1}{2} - (-2\frac{1}{8})$

EXERCISE 11.5

Solve each problem, writing answers in simplest form.

1. $\frac{3}{8} - \frac{7}{8}$

2. $\frac{1}{2} - \frac{8}{16}$

3. $-\frac{7}{8} - (-\frac{3}{16})$

4. $-\frac{1}{6} - \frac{1}{2}$

5. $\frac{5}{8} - (1\frac{1}{4})$

6. $\frac{6}{7} - \frac{5}{3}$

7. $\frac{3}{5} - (\frac{4}{5})$

8. $-\frac{1}{2} - (-\frac{7}{8})$

9. $-\frac{7}{8} - (-\frac{1}{2})$

10. $-5\frac{7}{8} - 3\frac{3}{4}$

11. $12\frac{1}{3} - 3$

12. $4\frac{1}{2} - 5\frac{2}{3}$

13. $2\frac{5}{7} - (-1\frac{2}{7})$

14. $-3\frac{3}{8} - 2\frac{1}{3}$

15. $-5\frac{1}{2} - (-3\frac{1}{7})$

EXERCISE 11.6

Solve each problem, writing answers in simplest form.

1. $y = \frac{3}{7} - \frac{1}{5}$

2. $-3\frac{1}{5} - \frac{3}{5} = x$

3. $4\frac{1}{8} - (-1\frac{3}{8}) = z$

4. $a = -7 - 2\frac{1}{8}$

5. $4\frac{1}{3} - 1\frac{1}{6} = m$

6. $n = 1\frac{3}{4} - (-4\frac{1}{2})$

7. $s = 2\frac{1}{2} - (-3\frac{7}{8})$

8. $w = 4\frac{1}{5} - 4\frac{9}{10}$

9. $t = -1\frac{3}{8} - 2\frac{3}{10}$

10. $v = \frac{4}{5} - (-2\frac{1}{8})$

11. $-6\frac{2}{3} - (-1\frac{1}{6}) = d$

12. $-5\frac{1}{2} - 4\frac{15}{16} = e$

13. $3\frac{2}{3} - 5\frac{1}{2} = g$

14. $-\frac{7}{8} - (2\frac{3}{16}) = h$

15. $-5\frac{7}{8} - 2\frac{3}{4} = k$

Multiplication of Rational Numbers

• The product of two rational numbers with the same sign is positive.

Examples

$$-\frac{1}{2} \cdot \left(-\frac{1}{4}\right)$$

$$-\frac{1}{2} \cdot -\frac{1}{4}$$

$$\frac{1}{8}$$

Two negative rational numbers.

$$c = \frac{1}{2} \cdot \frac{1}{4}$$

$$c = \frac{1}{8}$$

Two positve rational numbers.

• The product of two rational numbers with different signs is negative.

Examples

$$4\frac{1}{3} \cdot \left(-2\frac{1}{2}\right)$$

$$4\frac{1}{3} \cdot -2\frac{1}{2}$$

$$\frac{13}{3} \cdot -\frac{5}{2}$$

$$-\frac{65}{6} = -10\frac{5}{6}$$

One negative and one positive rational numbers.

$$d = -2\frac{1}{4}\left(3\frac{1}{5}\right)$$

$$d = -2\frac{1}{4} \cdot 3\frac{1}{5}$$

$$d = -\frac{9}{4} \cdot \frac{16}{5}$$

$$d = -\frac{144}{20}$$

$$d = -7\frac{1}{5}$$

One negative and one positive rational numbers.

EXERCISE 11.7

State whether the product of each problem is positive (+) or negative (–). Solving each problem and reducing to simplest terms is optional.

1. $\left(-\frac{3}{4}\right)\left(\frac{1}{3}\right)$

2. $-\frac{1}{2} \cdot 4$

3. $\frac{3}{8} \cdot \left(-\frac{1}{6}\right)$

4. $\left(-4\frac{1}{8}\right)\left(-2\frac{1}{16}\right)$

5. $7 \cdot \left(\frac{1}{3}\right)$

6. $-10\frac{1}{2} \cdot \left(-\frac{5}{2}\right)$

7. $8\frac{1}{2}\left(-3\frac{1}{3}\right)$

8. $-10 \cdot \frac{1}{10}$

9. $\frac{4}{5}\left(-\frac{5}{4}\right)$

10. $\left(2\frac{1}{2}\right)\left(2\frac{1}{7}\right)$

11. $-\frac{5}{6}\left(-1\right)$

12. $5 \cdot \left(5\frac{1}{6}\right)$

EXERCISE 11.8

Solve each problem, reducing to simplest form.

1. $y = 5\left(-\frac{1}{3}\right)$

2. $\frac{1}{3}(-5) = w$

3. $z = \left(\frac{1}{4}\right)\left(\frac{1}{7}\right)$

4. $v = -\frac{5}{6}\left(-\frac{2}{5}\right)$

5. $s = \frac{7}{8} \cdot -\frac{2}{3}$

6. $r = \left(-2\frac{1}{3}\right)\left(-\frac{3}{4}\right)$

7. $\left(3\frac{1}{4}\right)\left(-2\frac{1}{3}\right) = p$

8. $m = 5\frac{1}{2} \cdot 3\frac{1}{2}$

9. $a = -\frac{3}{4} \cdot -1\frac{7}{8}$

10. $b = -16\left(-\frac{3}{8}\right)$

11. $c = \left(-6\frac{1}{3}\right)\left(3\frac{2}{5}\right)$

12. $d = 3\frac{1}{3} \cdot 3\frac{1}{3}$

13. $\left(-\frac{7}{8}\right)\left(2\frac{4}{7}\right) = g$

14. $h = \left(3\frac{3}{4}\right)\left(4\frac{2}{5}\right)$

15. $k = \left(-\frac{3}{5}\right)\left(\frac{5}{3}\right)$

16. $f = -\frac{1}{5} \cdot 2\frac{1}{6}$

17. $\left(-5\frac{1}{2}\right)\left(-2\frac{2}{3}\right) = n$

18. $25\left(-\frac{1}{2}\right) = x$

Division of Rational Numbers

•Division of rational numbers with the same sign is positive.

Examples

$$a = \frac{3}{4} \div \frac{1}{2}$$

$$a = \frac{3}{4} \cdot \frac{2}{1}$$

$$a = \frac{6}{4}$$

$$a = 1\frac{1}{2}$$

Two positive rational numbers.
Remember that division can be changed to
multiplication by flipping the second number
(making it a reciprocal) and multiplying.

$$-\frac{3}{4} \div -\frac{1}{2}$$

$$-\frac{3}{4} \cdot -\frac{2}{1}$$

$$\frac{6}{4} = 1\frac{1}{2}$$

Two negative rational numbers.

•Division of two rational numbers with different signs is negative.

Examples

$$b = -\frac{3}{4} \div \frac{1}{2}$$

$$b = -\frac{3}{4} \cdot \frac{2}{1}$$

$$b = -\frac{6}{4}$$

$$b = -1\frac{1}{2}$$

One negative and one positive rational numbers.

$$\frac{3}{4} \div -\frac{1}{2}$$

$$\frac{3}{4} \cdot -\frac{2}{1}$$

$$-\frac{6}{4} = -1\frac{1}{2}$$

One positive and one negative rational numbers.

EXERCISE 11.9

State whether the product of each problem is positive (+) or negative (–). Solving each problem and reducing to simplest terms is optional.

1. $x = \frac{5}{8} \div \frac{1}{3}$

2. $\frac{1}{2} \div (-\frac{3}{5})$

3. $-\frac{3}{4} \div 7$

4. $m = -\frac{1}{6} \div 2\frac{1}{2}$

5. $5\frac{1}{4} \div -2\frac{1}{2}$

6. $(-4\frac{1}{3}) \div (-1\frac{1}{4})$

7. $y = 18 \div -\frac{5}{8}$

8. $(3\frac{1}{7}) \div (3\frac{1}{7})$

9. $z = -4 \div \frac{1}{2}$

EXERCISE 11.10

Solve each problem, reducing to simplest form.

1. $a = -\frac{1}{10} \div (-\frac{1}{30})$

2. $r = 49 \div -\frac{7}{8}$

3. $t = -\frac{1}{14} \div \frac{5}{7}$

4. $3\frac{3}{4} \div 2\frac{1}{3} = s$

5. $6\frac{5}{6} \div 2\frac{1}{3} = v$

6. $w = -12 \div \frac{6}{7}$

7. $x = -\frac{7}{8} \div \frac{2}{3}$

8. $y = (-\frac{4}{5}) \div (-\frac{3}{4})$

9. $-6\frac{1}{2} \div 1\frac{1}{5} = z$

10. $3\frac{1}{4} \div 2\frac{1}{2} = c$

11. $d = 3\frac{1}{8} \div 2$

12. $e = -5\frac{1}{4} \div -\frac{2}{3}$

13. $g = (-\frac{16}{3}) \div (\frac{3}{4})$

14. $h = 2\frac{7}{8} \div \frac{7}{8}$

15. $j = (4\frac{1}{8}) \div (2\frac{1}{16})$

Ratio, Proportion and Percent

A **ratio** is a comparison of two numbers by division. A ratio can be written in several ways:

$$2 : 3 \qquad 2 \text{ to } 3 \qquad \frac{2}{3} \qquad 2/3$$

In mathematics, ratios are most often written in fraction form. Ratios, like regular fractions, can be simplified. As long as the same number is divided into both the numerator and denominator (except zero), the resulting reduction maintains the same relationship between the ratio numbers.

The numbers making up ratios can also be enlarged and still maintain the same relationship between the ratio numbers.

Examples

Reducing ratio numbers and maintaining ratio equivalency.

$$\frac{75}{100} \div \frac{25}{25} = \frac{3}{4}$$

$$\frac{88}{99} \div \frac{11}{11} = \frac{8}{9}$$

Enlarging ratio numbers and maintaining ratio equivalency.

$$\frac{3}{4} \ 9 \ \frac{15}{15} = \frac{45}{60}$$

$$\frac{2}{3} \ 9 \ \frac{5}{5} = \frac{10}{15}$$

EXERCISE 12.1

Change each of the following ratios to a fraction form and reduce when necessary.

1. 4 out of 5 people
2. 49 out of 50 pennies
3. 10 women out of a group of 22 people

4. 8 eggs to a dozen
5. 3 miles to 5 hours
6. $6 to 25 cents

7. 25 days out of a year
8. 40 years out of a century
9. 30 minute out of 4 hours

EXERCISE 12.2

The distance between each point is labeled. Express the ratio between each point in simplest terms.

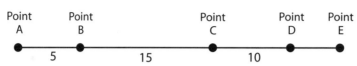

| Point A | Point B | Point C | Point D | Point E |

1. AB : BC

2. BC : CD

3. AB : AC

4. CD : AB

5. BC : AD

6. BC : BD

EXERCISE 12.3

Complete these ratio reductions.

1. $\frac{6}{12} \div \frac{a}{6} = \frac{1}{2}$

2. $\frac{14}{16} \div \frac{2}{b} = \frac{7}{8}$

3. $\frac{15}{40} \div \frac{c}{5} = \frac{3}{8}$

4. $\frac{18}{21} \div \frac{3}{3} = \frac{d}{7}$

5. $\frac{15}{25} \div \frac{5}{5} = \frac{3}{e}$

6. $\frac{20}{28} \div \frac{f}{4} = \frac{g}{7}$

7. $\frac{24}{60} \div \frac{12}{h} = \frac{2}{j}$

8. $\frac{18}{81} \div \frac{k}{9} = \frac{m}{9}$

9. $\frac{32}{12} \div \frac{4}{n} = \frac{8}{p}$

10. $\frac{6}{24} \div \frac{r}{6} = \frac{1}{s}$

11. $\frac{14}{21} \div \frac{7}{t} = \frac{v}{7}$

12. $\frac{11}{22} \div \frac{w}{x} = \frac{1}{z}$

13. $\frac{y}{27} \div \frac{9}{9} = \frac{2}{3}$

14. $\frac{10}{x} \div \frac{10}{10} = \frac{1}{4}$

15. $\frac{a}{300} \div \frac{12}{12} = \frac{3}{25}$

EXERCISE 12.4

Complete these ratio enlargements.

1. $\frac{3}{1} \cdot \frac{7}{7} = \frac{a}{b}$

2. $\frac{3}{5} \cdot \frac{5}{5} = \frac{e}{f}$

3. $\frac{4}{5} \cdot \frac{g}{6} = \frac{24}{30}$

4. $\frac{8}{9} \cdot \frac{3}{h} = \frac{24}{27}$

5. $\frac{1}{2} \cdot \frac{15}{j} = \frac{k}{30}$

6. $\frac{3}{8} \cdot \frac{m}{13} = \frac{39}{n}$

7. $\frac{13}{21} \cdot \frac{p}{q} = \frac{52}{84}$

8. $\frac{3}{4} \cdot \frac{r}{s} = \frac{33}{44}$

9. $\frac{5}{7} \cdot \frac{6}{t} = \frac{30}{u}$

10. $\frac{7}{16} \cdot \frac{v}{4} = \frac{w}{64}$

11. $\frac{6}{12} \cdot \frac{x}{y} = \frac{24}{z}$

12. $\frac{24}{9} \cdot \frac{a}{b} = \frac{c}{90}$

Proportion

A **proportion** names two equivalent ratios and can be written several different ways.

$$7 : 8 = 35 : 40 \qquad\qquad 7 \text{ is to } 8 \text{ as } 35 \text{ is to } 40 \qquad\qquad \frac{7}{8} = \frac{35}{40}$$

An easy method to tell if two ratios are equivalent is by multiplication of cross products.

$$\frac{3}{4} \times \frac{18}{24} \qquad \begin{array}{l} 4 \cdot 18 = 72 \\ 3 \cdot 24 = 72 \end{array} \qquad \text{Equivalent: } \frac{3}{4} = \frac{18}{24}$$

$$\frac{2}{3} \times \frac{10}{16} \qquad \begin{array}{l} 3 \cdot 10 = 30 \\ 2 \cdot 16 = 32 \end{array} \qquad \text{Not equivalent: } \frac{2}{3} \neq \frac{10}{16}$$

If cross products are equal, the ratios are equivalent.

EXERCISE 12.5

Determine if these ratios are proportional (equivalent) or not proportional (non-equivalent). Place an equal sign (=) for proportional ratios and an unequal sign ($\neq$) for ratios that are not proportional.

1. $\frac{3}{8}$	$\frac{6}{16}$		**6.** $\frac{1.2}{1.6}$	$\frac{3}{4}$		**11.** $\frac{59}{9}$	$\frac{10}{3}$
2. $\frac{4}{5}$	$\frac{13}{15}$		**7.** $\frac{.5}{1}$	$\frac{5}{10}$		**12.** $\frac{12}{8}$	$\frac{2}{3}$
3. $\frac{7}{5}$	$\frac{25}{4}$		**8.** $\frac{28}{22}$	$\frac{8}{6}$		**13.** $\frac{15}{2}$	$\frac{45}{6}$
4. $\frac{6}{15}$	$\frac{42}{105}$		**9.** $\frac{6}{8}$	$\frac{2}{3}$		**14.** $\frac{3}{12}$	$\frac{4}{8}$
5. $\frac{8}{9}$	$\frac{16}{17}$		**10.** $\frac{4}{5}$	$\frac{12}{15}$		**15.** $\frac{25}{39}$	$\frac{180}{125}$

How can proportions between ratios be kept if part of a ratio is missing? Cross multiplication can help.

$$\frac{6}{15} = \frac{?}{75}$$

Examples

$\frac{6}{15} : \frac{x}{75}$ *x represents a missing value that would complete the proportion.*

$\frac{6}{15} \diagdown\!\!\!\!\diagup \frac{x}{75}$ $15x = 450$

$x = 30$

$\frac{6}{15} : \frac{30}{75}$

$\frac{2}{3} : \frac{b}{12}$ *b represents a missing value that would complete the proportion.*

$\frac{2}{3} \diagdown\!\!\!\!\diagup \frac{b}{12}$ $3b = 24$

$b = 8$

$\frac{2}{3} : \frac{8}{12}$

$\frac{15}{20} : \frac{9}{z}$ *z represents a missing value that would complete the proportion.*

$\frac{15}{20} \diagdown\!\!\!\!\diagup \frac{9}{z}$ $15z = 180$

$z = 12$

$\frac{15}{20} : \frac{9}{12}$

EXERCISE 12.6

Find the missing ratio that completes each proportion.

1. $\frac{3}{8} = \frac{b}{24}$

2. $\frac{12}{16} = \frac{c}{8}$

3. $\frac{m}{12} = \frac{7}{12}$

4. $\frac{c}{18} = \frac{9}{54}$

5. $\frac{90}{x} = \frac{30}{11}$

6. $\frac{360}{15} = \frac{72}{w}$

7. $\frac{9}{8} = \frac{144}{h}$

8. $\frac{45}{d} = \frac{5}{6}$

9. $\frac{7}{11} = \frac{84}{a}$

10. $\frac{5}{13} = \frac{10}{v}$

11. $\frac{12}{8} = \frac{9}{t}$

12. $\frac{27}{5} = \frac{81}{e}$

Percent

Percent is a ratio that compares a number to 100. A percent can be gained from fractions and decimals. Knowing how to move between fractions, decimals, and percents is always useful.

•Decimals to Percents—and back again.

To compare a decimal number to 100, the decimal point is moved two (2) places to the right and the percent sign (%) is added. Zeros are inserted when necessary. For instance, the decimal number .23 when converted to a percent is 23%.

Examples

Decimal	Move right 2 places	Add percent sign	
.47	.47	47%	
.02	.02	2%	
4.5	4.5	450%	*Fill-in 1 zero.*
6	6	600%	*Fill-in 2 zeros.*
12.72	12.72	1272%	
.309	30.9	30.9%	

EXERCISE 12.7

Which is the correct conversion to a percent?

1. .0524 = .524% 5.24% 52.4%
2. 1.4 = 1.4% 14% 140%
3. 3 = 3% 30% 300%
4. 4.962 = 49.63% 496.2% 4963%

5. 62.58 = .62.58% 625.8% 6258%
6. .0032 = .032% .32% 3.2%
7. 5.4 + 2.3 = 77% 770% neither
8. 12.5 – 7.6 = 49% 4.9% neither

EXERCISE 12.8

Changing back. Return these percents to decimals numbers.

1. 68%
2. 1%
3. 5.367%
4. 9.6%
5. 6%

6. 7000%
7. 99.9%
8. .06%
9. 52.74%
10. .9%

11. 46.22%
12. 29.8%
13. .027%
14. 1467%
15. 176%

• Fractions to Percents—and back again.

To convert from a fraction to a percent: 1) convert any mixed numbers to improper fractions; 2) divide the numerator of the fraction by its denominator; 3) multiply by 100 (simply move the decimal point two places to the right); and, 4) add a percent sign (%). You will see a few shortcuts in the examples to follow.

Examples

Fraction Whole number	Divide	Move decimal or multiply by 100	%	
$3\frac{3}{8} = \frac{27}{8}$	$27 \div 8$	3.375	337.5%	*Note improper fraction.*
		or		
		$3.375 \cdot 100 = 337.5\%$		
$\frac{3}{5}$	$3 \div 5$	$.60$	60%	
$\frac{27}{100}$	$27 \div 100$	$.27$	27%	
9	*No division necessary.*	$9.$	900%	*Fill-in 2 zeros.*

EXERCISE 12.9

Change each fraction to a percent. When necessary, round any decimal to the nearest tenth.

1. $\frac{1}{10}$ **6.** $1\frac{7}{8}$ **11.** $\frac{13}{20}$

2. $\frac{1}{2}$ **7.** $4\frac{31}{100}$ **12.** $\frac{16}{12}$

3. $\frac{1}{9}$ **8.** $\frac{4}{5}$ **13.** $6\frac{2}{3}$

4. $\frac{1}{8}$ **9.** $6\frac{1}{2}$ **14.** $\frac{7}{18}$

5. $\frac{1}{20}$ **10.** $9\frac{1}{7}$ **15.** $1\frac{11}{30}$

EXERCISE 12.10

Changing back. Return these percents to fractions. Reduce to lowest terms.

1. 55%   **6.** 57%   **11.** 325%

2. 2%   **7.** 120%   **12.** 81%

3. 1430%   **8.** 95%   **13.** 700%

4. 60%   **9.** 80%   **14.** 5%

5. 75%   **10.** 250%   **15.** 12.5%

EXERCISE 12.11

Review: Pulling it all together. Complete each column. Reduce to lowest terms when necessary.
Round decimals to the nearest hundredth when necessary.

	Percent	Fraction	Decimal
1.	25%	_____	_____
2.	_____	$\frac{37}{100}$	_____
3.	_____	_____	.06
4.	_____	$\frac{1}{8}$	_____
5.	_____	_____	.32
6.	50%	_____	_____
7.	_____	$\frac{4}{5}$	_____
8.	39%	_____	_____
9.	_____	$\frac{16}{25}$	_____
10.	220%	_____	_____
11.	_____	_____	.01
12.	_____	$5\frac{3}{4}$	_____
13.	4.5%	_____	_____
14.	_____	_____	.125
15.	_____	$\frac{1}{50}$	_____
16.	1000%	_____	_____
17.	_____	_____	.2
18.	_____	7	_____
19.	45%	_____	_____
20.	_____	_____	.9

Mastery Test

A. Circle the numbers that are factors of the first number.

1. 8: 2, 4, 6, 9

2. 20: 15, 10, 20

3. 19: 5, 9, 10, 19

4. 28: 3, 5, 7, 9

5. 45: 3, 6, 9, 12

6. 22: 1, 2, 3, 7

B. Reduce these composite numbers to the product of prime factors.

7. 84

8. 90

9. 64

C. Find the Greatest Common Factor (GCF) and Least Common Multiple (LCM) in each problem.

10. 12, 18

11. 30, 45

12. 24, 18

13. 12, 22

14. 9, 21, 36

15. 8, 80, 100

D. Simplify each problem as an exponential expression (do not evaluate).

16. $9 \cdot 9 \cdot 9 =$

17. 5 squared =

18. 10 to the fifth power =

19. $(y^3)^4 =$

20. $5^4 \div 5^4 =$

21. $a^4 \div a^3 =$

22. $3y^2 + 10y^2 =$

23. $(2b^2)(5b^3) =$

24. $10c^5 \div 2c^2 =$

E. Combine these variables and order them correctly.

25. $w \cdot x \cdot y$

26. $\frac{72m}{12m}$

27. $8r \cdot 7st$

28. $32g - 6 - 5g$

29. $2 \cdot 2 \cdot 2cd$

30. $8k \cdot 8k + 5$

31. $v^2 \div vw$

32. $3x \cdot 4y$

33. $60m^2n \div 12m$

34. $23w + 17x + 7 + y$

35. $14p - 15q$

36. $7 \cdot 6c \cdot 2$

F. Properties.

37. Use the Commutatve Property to reorder and prove this problem: $12 + 6 + y =$

38. Use the Associative Property to regroup and prove this problem: $27 \cdot (4 \cdot 5) =$

39. Use the Distributive Property to distribute and prove this problem: $3(4 + 7 - 8) =$

40. State the property (Commutative, Associative, or Distributive) that is illustrated in each problem.

a. $7(4 + 3) + 10 = 7(4) + 7(3) + 10$

b. $(\frac{1}{4} + \frac{1}{2}) + \frac{3}{4} = \frac{1}{4} + (\frac{1}{2} + \frac{3}{4})$

c. $4 + 8 + 12 = 12 + 8 + 4$

G. Integer with Rational Numbers. Solve each problem.

41. $-7 + -2 + -7$

42. $x = 6 - (-83)$

43. $-5 \cdot -17$

44. $\frac{-5}{25}$

45. $b = \frac{1}{10} \div (-\frac{1}{30})$

46. $-11(27) = m$

47. $\frac{(-4 + 6)\,(-2)}{5(-3) - (-3)}$

48. $a = -4\frac{1}{3} \cdot (2\frac{1}{2})$

49. $-\frac{1}{4} + (-\frac{5}{8})$

50. $-36 \div (-9) - 4(2)$

51. $z = 2\frac{1}{2} - 4\frac{5}{12}$

52. $(5 \cdot 6)\,(-12 \div -6)$

H. Ratio, Proportion and Percent

Change each of the following fractions to percents. When necessary round to the nearest tenth.

53. $4\frac{51}{100}$

54. $4\frac{2}{3}$

55. $\frac{1}{8}$

56. $1\frac{7}{8}$

57. $\frac{7}{18}$

58. $\frac{1}{10}$

Change each of the following decimals to percents.

59. .0278

60. 7

61. 4.52

62. .006

63. .9

64. .384

Supply the missing fraction, decimal or percent. Reduce fractions to lowest terms. Round decimals to the nearest hundredth when necessary.

	Fraction	Decimal	Percent
65.	$5\frac{3}{4}$	____	____
66.	____	.002	____
67.	____	____	4.5%
68.	$\frac{1}{20}$	____	____
69.	____	.45	____
70.	____	____	87.7%

GLOSSARY OF

Terms

Associative Property The grouping in which numbers are added or multiplied does not change their result. For example: $(2 \cdot 3) \cdot 4 = 2 \cdot (3 \cdot 4)$.

Base Number A number used as a factor a given number of times. For example: in 4^2, 4 is the base number.

Coefficient A number in front of a variable. For example: in the expressions $10xy$ and x, 10 is the coefficient in the expression $10xy$, and 1 is the understood coefficient for the expression of x.

Composite Numbers A whole number greater than 1 that has at least one factor besides itself and 1.

Commutative Property The order in which numbers are added or multiplied does not change their results. For example: $13 + 26 + 2 = 2 + 26 + 13$.

Distributive Property When the sum of two numbers contained within parentheses is to be multiplied by another number, the other number can be used (distributed) with each of the numbers within, multiplying each one separately. For example: $2(3 + 4) = 2 \cdot 3 + 2 \cdot 4$.

Exponent The number of times a base number is used as a factor. For instance: in the expression 4^2, 4 is used twice as a factor.

Expression Any collection of numbers, variables, parentheses, or operations. For example: $-6x - 10y + 7y + 10$.

Factor Quantities (sometimes numbers; sometimes variables) that when multiplied together yield a product. For example: 2 and 7 are factors of 14.

Formula An equation that states a fact or rule.

Greatest Common Factor (GCF) The largest number that is the factor of two or more numbers. For example: The GCF of 12 and 18 is 6.

Integers Numbers, their opposites, and zero. Positive integers are numbers greater than zero; and, negative integers are numbers less than zero. For example: 6, –6, 0.

Irrational Numbers Numbers that cannot be represented as exact ratios of two integers. For example: square root of 2, pi.

Like Terms Numerals, variables or a combination of numerals and variables that are similar. For example: in the expression $-6x - 10y + 7y + x$, $-6x$ and x, and $-10y$ and $7y$ are like terms.

Lowest Common Multiple (LCM) The smallest number that is a factor of two or more numbers (zero excepted). For example: The LCM of 3 and 5 is 15.

Operations Changes to quantities (e.g., numbers, variables) using rules or symbols (e.g., +, −, x, ÷).

Order of Operations Rules that are used for the order in which operations (e.g., +, −, x, ÷) are performed to reach an answer.

Percent A ratio that compares a number to 100.

Power The product of a number multiplied by itself. For example: $5 \cdot 5 \cdot 5$, or 5^3, is five to the third power.

Prime Factorization Whole numbers reduced to the product of prime numbers. For example: The composite number 72 is composed of the prime numbers $2 \cdot 2 \cdot 2 \cdot 3 \cdot 3$.

Prime Number A whole number greater than 1 that has only 1 and itself as factors.

Properties Qualities and relationships that explain numbers.

Proportion Two equivalent ratios.

Ratio A comparison of two numbers by division.

Rational Number A number that can be named in a fraction form with a numerator and with a denominator that is an integer (the denominator cannot be zero).

Real Numbers All rational and irrational numbers.

Signed Numbers See integers.

Terms Parts of an expression. For instance: in the expression $-6x -10y + 7y + x$, $-6x$, $-10y$, $7y$, and x are terms.

Variable A symbol representing a missing number. For example: $23x$, where x represents a missing value.

Whole Number A positive number greater than zero.

Answers

Order of Operations 1.1, page 6.

1. 3	**6.** 25	**11.** 6	**16.** 75
2. 16	**7.** 27	**12.** 4	**17.** 2
3. 12	**8.** 5	**13.** 3	**18.** 84
4. 19	**9.** 7	**14.** 10	**19.** 10
5. 0	**10.** 18	**15.** 33	**20.** 11

Order of Operations 1.2, page 6.

1. Step 1: Parentheses
Step 2: Exponent
Step 3: Multiplication
Step 4: Subtraction

2. Step 1: Parentheses (twice)
Step 3: Multiplication

3. Step 3: Multiplication
Step 4: Subtraction
Step 4: Addition

4. Step 3: Division
Step 3: Multiplication
Step 4: Addition

Factors 2.1, page 8.

1. $1 \cdot 10, 2 \cdot 5$
1, 2, 5, 10

2. $1 \cdot 42, 2 \cdot 21, 3 \cdot 14, 6 \cdot 7$
1, 2, 3, 6, 7, 14, 21, 42

3. $1 \cdot 60, 2 \cdot 30, 3 \cdot 20,$
$4 \cdot 15, 5 \cdot 12, 6 \cdot 10$
1, 2, 3, 4, 5, 6, 10, 12
15, 20, 30, 60

4. $1 \cdot 16, 2 \cdot 8, 4 \cdot 4$
1, 2, 4, 8, 16

5. $1 \cdot 48, 2 \cdot 24, 3 \cdot 16,$
$4 \cdot 12, 6 \cdot 8$
1, 2, 3, 4, 6, 8, 12, 16,
24, 48

6. $1 \cdot 25, 5 \cdot 5$
1, 5, 25

7. $1 \cdot 20, 2 \cdot 10, 4 \cdot 5$
1, 2, 4, 5, 10, 20

8. $1 \cdot 110, 2 \cdot 55, 5 \cdot 22, 10 \cdot 11$
1, 2, 5, 10, 11, 22, 55, 110

9. $1 \cdot 333, 3 \cdot 111$
1, 3, 111, 333

10. $1 \cdot 7$
1, 7

11. Yes, divides evenly.
12. Yes, divides evenly.
13. Yes, divides evenly.
14. No, doesn't divide evenly.
15. Yes, divides evenly.
16. Yes, divides evenly.
17. Yes, divides evenly.
18. No, doesn't divide evenly.
19. 6: 1, 2, 3
20. 17: 17
21. 37: None
22. 20: 1, 5, 10, 20
23. 30: 3, 5, 15
24. 45: 3, 9
25. 27: 1, 3, 9
26. 28: 7
27. 105: 5, 105
28. 128: 8, 32, 64

Prime and Composite Numbers 3.1, page 10.

Composite numbers may vary, but prime numbers remain the same.

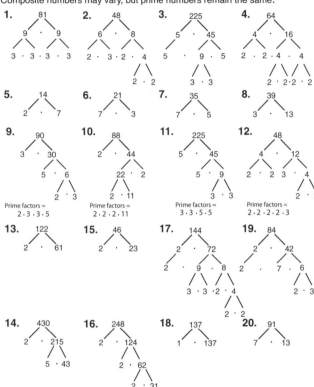

Prime and Composite Numbers 3.2, page 11.

1. $81 = 3 \cdot 3 \cdot 3 \cdot 3$	**8.** $39 = 3 \cdot 13$	**15.** $46 = 2 \cdot 23$
2. $48 = 2 \cdot 2 \cdot 2 \cdot 2 \cdot 3$	**9.** $90 = 2 \cdot 3 \cdot 3 \cdot 5$	**16.** $248 = 2 \cdot 2 \cdot 2 \cdot 31$
3. $225 = 3 \cdot 3 \cdot 5 \cdot 5$	**10.** $88 = 2 \cdot 2 \cdot 2 \cdot 11$	**17.** $144 = 2 \cdot 2 \cdot 2 \cdot 2 \cdot 3 \cdot 3$
4. $64 = 2 \cdot 2 \cdot 2 \cdot 2 \cdot 2 \cdot 2$	**11.** $225 = 3 \cdot 3 \cdot 5 \cdot 5$	**18.** $137 = 1 \cdot 137$
5. $14 = 2 \cdot 7$	**12.** $\cdot 2 \cdot 2 \cdot 2 \cdot 3$	**19.** $84 = 2 \cdot 2 \cdot 3 \cdot 7$
6. $21 = 3 \cdot 7$	**13.** $122 = 2 \cdot 61$	**20.** $91 = 7 \cdot 13$
7. $35 = 5 \cdot 7$	**14.** $430 = 2 \cdot 5 \cdot 43$	

Greatest Common Factor 4.1, page 13.

1. 6,4: 2	**5.** 18, 41: 6	**9.** 28, 42: 14
2. 36, 45: 9	**6.** 56, 84: 28	**10.** 64, 28: 4
3. 100, 25: 25	**7.** 24, 16: 8	**11.** 90, 126: 18
4. 8, 12: 4	**8.** 64, 80: 16	**12.** 66, 88: 22

Greatest Common Factor 4.2, page 14.

1. 3, 7: 1	**8.** 36, 45: 9	**15.** 19, 57: 19
2. 18, 30: 6	**9.** 11, 21: 1	**16.** 6, 8, 4: 2
3. 15, 35: 5	**10.** 60, 36: 12	**17.** 80, 10, 15: 5
4. 6, 36: 6	**11.** 30, 50: 10	**18.** 36, 24, 48: 12
5. 42, 28: 14	**12.** 81, 27: 27	**19.** 12, 27, 42: 3
6. 20, 35: 5	**13.** 54, 66: 6	
7. 24, 40: 8	**14.** 64, 40: 8	

Greatest Common Factor 4.3, Page 14.

1. 4, 12: 4   **4.** 27, 39: 3   **7.** 84, 42: 42
2. 9, 18: 9   **5.** 48, 72: 24   **8.** 30, 50: 10
3. 28, 36: 4   **6.** 24, 32: 8

Exponents 5.1, Page 15.

1. 9^7 **5.** 132^2 **9.** 15^4
2. 3^2 **6.** 17^5 **10.** 2^6
3. 4^3 **7.** 10^2 **11.** 7^3
4. 8^1 **8.** 8^5 **12.** 9^4

Exponents 5.2, Page 16.

1. 9   **6.** 49   **11.** 729
2. 32   **7.** 125   **12.** 121
3. 27   **8.** 16   **13.** 1296
4. 16   **9.** 256   **14.** 27,000
5. 1   **10.** 100   **15.** 15

Exponents 5.3, Page 16.

1. 5^2 **4.** 2^6 **7.** 10^7
2. 3^4 **5.** 7^3 **8.** 5^4
3. 10^4 **6.** 5^5 **9.** 2^8

Least Common Multiple 6.1, Page 18.

1. 4, 6: 12   **6.** 2, 10: 10   **11.** 12, 32: 96
2. 12, 16: 48   **7.** 10, 15: 30   **12.** 18, 24: 72
3. 5, 6: 30   **8.** 7, 6: 42   **13.** 27, 36: 108
4. 6, 8: 24   **9.** 15, 35: 105   **14.** 21, 48: 336
5. 4, 9: 36   **10.** 8, 20: 40   **15.** 24, 56: 168

Least Common Multiple 6.2, Page 18.

1. 8,9: 72   **5.** 6, 8, 12: 24   **9.** 8, 10, 25: 200
2. 15, 75: 75   **6.** 7, 21, 84: 84   **10.** 12, 16, 24: 48
3. 14, 21: 42   **7.** 9, 12, 15: 180   **11.** 14, 18, 21: 126
4. 3, 4, 6: 12   **8.** 6, 9, 15: 90   **12.** 20, 36, 48: 720

Least Common Multiple 6.3, Page 18.

1. 21, 36: GCF 3; LCM 252   **5.** 15, 36, 75: GCF 3; LCM 900
2. 18, 24: GCF 6; LCM 72   **6.** 6, 60, 100: GCF 2; LCM 300
3. 6, 9, 12: GCF 3; LCM 36   **7.** 6, 9, 18: GCF 3; LCM 18
4. 9, 21, 36: GCF 3; LCM 252   **8.** 14, 42, 49: GCF 7; LCM 294

Variables 7.1, Page 19.

1. 21   **6.** 143   **11.** 47
2. 18   **7.** 34   **12.** 43
3. 24   **8.** 18   **13.** 15
4. 7   **9.** 6   **14.** 0
5. 18   **10.** 22   **15.** 66

Variables 7.2, Page 20.

1. x = 18   **4.** m = 59   **7.** s = 713
2. a = 23   **5.** n = 72   **8.** g = 2634
3. d = 11   **6.** y = 339   **9.** w = 84

10. k = 946   **13.** k = 353   **16.** z = 225
11. v = 36   **14.** z = 29   **17.** y = 536
12. h = 850   **15.** c = 2013   **18.** t = 998

Variable 7.3, Page 20.

1. 19m   **6.** 4a + c   **11.** 5m − 4n + 6
2. 100x   **7.** 9z   **12.** 3r + 4s − 17
3. 52a + 5c   **8.** 32c + 4d − 6   **13.** −c + 13d + 1
4. no change   **9.** e + 4f − 9g   **14.** 3c + 2x + xy
5. 11d + 4g   **10.** 55a + 9   **15.** −a + 9ab + bc

Variables 7.4, Page 22.

1. ab   **7.** 12yz   **13.** cdg
2. 75c   **8.** 248h   **14.** $8c^2$
3. $120x^2$ **9.** 225   **15.** 84b
4. 92d   **10.** 165kj   **16.** w^3
5. m^2 **11.** $2v^2$ **17.** 27abc
6. 144rs   **12.** 130st   **18.** $40m^3$

Variables 7.5, Page 23.

1. 1   **6.** $8\frac{m}{n}$ **11.** a^2
2. 2d   **7.** $\frac{25x}{y}$ **12.** $\frac{3z}{p}$
3. $\frac{g}{h}$ **8.** 15b   **13.** 1
4. 3   **9.** 5ab   **14.** 12
5. 3a   **10.** v   **15.** $9n^2$

Variables 7.6, Page 23.

1. 3a + 5b   **9.** 16x + 7xy   **17.** $4055s^3$
2. 3   **10.** 11a + 27   **18.** $225c^3$
3. c   **11.** 6c + 19d + 12   **19.** 216d
4. tuv   **12.** 36c   **20.** $\frac{w}{v}$
5. 42n   **13.** $\frac{k}{5m}$ **21.** $160w^2$
6. 3c − 7d   **14.** 8a + 7c + 25   **22.** $\frac{d}{3b}$
7. 1   **15.** 56rst   **23.** $\frac{42}{y}$
8. $\frac{a}{c}$ **16.** 7e   **24.** $64g^2h$

Properties 8.1, Page 24.

Answers will vary.

1. 6 + 15 + x   **4.** 5·7·8·3   **7.** 35x·10w
2. 5c·a   **5.** 5·4·3   **8.** b + a
3. 8 + 6 + 4   **6.** y + 17   **9.** 9 + 1 + 13

Properties 8.2, Page 24.

1. Reordering the numbers does change the results:
$1 \div 2 \neq 2$. The Commutative Property does not
hold true with division.

PROPERTIES 8.3, PAGE 25.

Answers may vary.

1. 78 + (4 + 7)   **4.** 27(5•7)   **7.** (5 + 7) + 6 + 4
2. (3•7)•2   **5.** (15 + 25) + 17   **8.** 7(5•8)•6
3. 32 + (6 + 9)   **6.** (10•19)•5   **9.** 12 + (15 + 16)

PROPERTIES 8.4, PAGE 25.

1. Regrouping the numbers does change the results:

24 ÷ (6 ÷ 2) ≠ 2.

PROPERTIES 8.5, PAGE 26.

1. 4(4 + 7) = 4(4) + 4(7)   **4.** 9(6 − 4) = 9•6 −9•4
2. 12(60 + 5) = 12(60) + 12(5)   **5.** 4(6 + 5 − 3) = 4(6) + 4(5) − 4(3)
3. 8(12 − 6) = 8(12) − 8(6)   **6.** 10(14 + 10) = 10•14 + 10•10

PROPERTIES 8.6, PAGE 26.

1. 4(4 + 7) = 4(4) + 4(7)   **4.** 9(6 − 4) = 9•6 −9•4
    4(11) = 16 + 28   9•2 = 54 − 36
      44 = 44   18 = 18
2. 12(60 + 5) = 12(60) + 12(5)   **5.** 4(6 + 5 − 3) = 4(6) + 4(5) − 4(3)
    12(65) = 720 + 60   4(8)= 24 + 20 −12
      780 = 780   32 = 32
3. 8(12 − 6) = 8(12) − 8(6)   **6.** 10(14 + 10) = 10•14 + 10•10
    8(6) = 96 − 48   10•24 = 140 + 100
      48 = 48   240 = 240

PROPERTIES 8.7, PAGE 26.

1. Commutative   **5.** Commutative   **9.** Distributive
2. Distributive   **6.** Commutative   **10.** Commutative
3. Distributive   **7.** Distributive   **11.** Associative
4. Associative   **8.** Associative   **12.** Commutative

PROPERTIES 8.8, PAGE 26.

1. Associative and Commutative.

INTEGERS 9.1, PAGE 27.

1. +7200 ft   **6.** −$27,000
2. −15 lbs   **7.** +57
3. +$1500   **8.** +34 lbs
4. −$124   **9.** +15 yds
5. −200 ft   **10.** −9

INTEGERS 9.2, PAGE 27.

1. +1   **5.** 0   **9.** −22
2. −1   **6.** −1   **10.** +17
3. −1   **7.** +4   **11.** +8
4. +7   **8.** −3   **12.** −1

INTEGERS 9.3, PAGE 28.

1. 9   **5.** −53   **9.** −24
2. −9   **6.** −53   **10.** −34
3. 22   **7.** 63   **11.** 36
4. −7   **8.** 24   **12.** −20

INTEGERS 9.4, PAGE 28.

1. b = −12   **4.** g = −107   **7.** w = −573
2. d = −14   **5.** m = −27   **8.** x = 160
3. a = 12   **6.** s = −102   **9.** z = −41

INTEGERS 9.5, PAGE 29.

1. −1   **5.** −9   **9.** −59
2. −3   **6.** −17   **10.** −97
3. −3   **7.** −7   **11.** −18
4. −1   **8.** −29   **12.** −134

INTEGERS 9.6, PAGE 29.

1. n = −1   **4.** x = 75   **7.** r = −19
2. a = −9   **5.** d = 15   **8.** w = −3
3. b = −26   **6.** p = −34   **9.** z = −2

INTEGERS 9.7, PAGE 29.

1. d = 15   **6.** a = 15   **11.** k = −565
2. c = −45   **7.** g = 335   **12.** c = −102
3. b = −69   **8.** m = −62   **13.** a = 49
4. r = 161   **9.** p = −14   **14.** e = 90
5. w = −119   **10.** y = 114   **15.** x = −103

INTEGERS 9.8, PAGE 30.

1. −   **7.** −   **13.** −
2. +   **8.** −   **14.** +
3. +   **9.** +   **15.** −
4. −   **10.** −   **16.** −
5. +   **11.** +   **17.** +
6. +   **12.** −   **18.** −

INTEGERS 9.9, PAGE 30.

1. −7   **7.** −1   **13.** −143
2. 11   **8.** −6   **14.** 397
3. 4   **9.** 15   **15.** −254
4. −4   **10.** −74   **16.** −143
5. 7   **11.** 143   **17.** 333
6. 20   **12.** −278   **18.** −93

INTEGERS 9.10, PAGE 30.

1. q = −1   **5.** p = −14   **9.** x = −22
2. a = 1   **6.** r = −12   **10.** y = −27
3. b = −6   **7.** s = 25   **11.** z = −635
4. k = −22   **8.** t = −84   **12.** a = −1172

INTEGERS 9.11, PAGE 31.

1. −   **6.** +   **11.** +
2. +   **7.** −   **12.** +
3. −   **8.** −   **13.** −
4. +   **9.** +   **14.** +
5. +   **10.** +   **15.** +

INTEGERS 9.12, PAGE 31.

1. −24   **6.** 555   **11.** 324
2. 100   **7.** 328   **12.** 324
3. 108   **8.** 7276   **13.** 1089
4. 54   **9.** 408   **14.** 126
5. 360   **10.** 480   **15.** 315

INTEGERS 9.13, PAGE 31.

1. b = −168 **6.** h = −120 **11.** r = 144
2. a = 60 **7.** k = 360 **12.** s = −216
3. c = −136 **8.** m = 81 **13.** t = −144
4. d = 180 **9.** n = −96 **14.** w = 70
5. g = −125 **10.** p = −76 **15.** x = −165

INTEGERS 9.14, PAGE 32.

1. + **6.** + **11.** +
2. − **7.** + **12.** −
3. − **8.** − **13.** −
4. − **9.** + **14.** −
5. − **10.** + **15.** −

INTEGERS 9.15, PAGE 32.

1. 9 **6.** 3 **11.** $\frac{1}{2}$
2. −9 **7.** 6 **12.** −21
3. −5 **8.** −3 **13.** −6
4. −5 **9.** $\frac{1}{3}$ **14.** $-3\frac{1}{2}$
5. −5 **10.** 3 **15.** $-\frac{1}{5}$

INTEGERS 9.16, PAGE 33.

1. 12 **6.** 9 **11.** −11
2. −4 **7.** 9 **12.** −21
3. −7 **8.** $13\frac{1}{2}$ **13.** −6
4. 5 **9.** −4 **14.** 1
5. −8 **10.** 32 **15.** $3\frac{1}{2}$

INTEGERS 9.17, PAGE 33.

1. a = −10 **4.** a = 48 **7.** w = −49
2. y = −8 **5.** b = −14 **8.** n = −12
3. z = −5 **6.** c = −13 **9.** s = $\frac{1}{4}$

INTEGERS 9.18, PAGE 34.

1. 9 **5.** −192 **9.** 20
2. −60 **6.** 180 **10.** 2
3. −40 **7.** 1 **11.** 10
4. −7 **8.** 6 **12.** −9

INTEGERS 9.19, PAGE 35.

1. −4 **7.** −29 **13.** 27
2. −13 **8.** −2 **14.** $\frac{3}{5}$
3. −20 **9.** 86 **15.** −5
4. 9 **10.** −4 **16.** −423
5. 60 **11.** $\frac{1}{3}$ **17.** −7
6. 34 **12.** −9 **18.** 2

MORE WITH EXPONENTS 10.1, PAGE 38.

1. c^3 **9.** 1 **17.** z^{10}
2. x^6 **10.** $2^7 \cdot 10^6$ **18.** $x^4 - y^4$
3. $3^3 \cdot 5$ **11.** 1 **19.** $3x^2 - 12x$
4. 7 **12.** $4g^5$ **20.** 6^{20}
5. m^2 **13.** x^{a+b} **21.** $3^{15} + 3^8$
6. $11x^3$ **14.** 3^8 **22.** 4^{38}
7. s **15.** 4^{10} **23.** $9x^4 - y^4$
8. 4^7 **16.** $10a^2 + b$ **24.** 3^{10}

MORE WITH EXPONENTS 10.2, PAGE 38.

1. $15b^3$ **5.** $30x^6$ **9.** $2x^3$
2. $3c^2$ **6.** 2 **10.** $127s^2$
3. $\frac{1}{16}$ **7.** $25x^2$ **11.** 2h
4. $3.36m^2$ **8.** $\frac{1}{2}r^2$ or $\frac{r^2}{2}$ **12.** $12w^7$

RATIONAL NUMBERS 11.1, PAGE 40.

1. + **5.** + **9.** +
2. − **6.** − **10.** −
3. − **7.** 0 **11.** +
4. − **8.** + **12.** −

RATIONAL NUMBERS 11.2, PAGE 40.

1. $\frac{5}{6}$ **5.** $-\frac{3}{5}$ **9.** $\frac{1}{4}$
2. $-\frac{1}{2}$ **6.** $\frac{1}{4}$ **10.** $-\frac{17}{24}$
3. −1 **7.** $-\frac{3}{5}$ **11.** $-\frac{5}{24}$
4. $-\frac{7}{10}$ **8.** $-\frac{1}{8}$ **12.** $\frac{3}{10}$

RATIONAL NUMBERS 11.3, PAGE 41.

1. x = $-1\frac{1}{3}$ **5.** w = $-1\frac{5}{24}$ **9.** n = $1\frac{1}{12}$
2. y = $5\frac{1}{4}$ **6.** m = $-10\frac{1}{6}$ **10.** z = $-6\frac{7}{8}$
3. a = $\frac{5}{6}$ **7.** g = $-1\frac{5}{8}$ **11.** r = $-2\frac{1}{8}$
4. b = $2\frac{1}{6}$ **8.** k = $2\frac{7}{8}$ **12.** q = $3\frac{5}{8}$

RATIONAL NUMBERS 11.4, PAGE 42.

1. $\frac{2}{3} + (-\frac{1}{3})$ **4.** $\frac{1}{3} + \frac{5}{6}$ **7.** $-2\frac{1}{4} + (-3\frac{3}{4})$
2. $-\frac{1}{8} + \frac{3}{4}$ **5.** $5 + \frac{5}{12}$ **8.** $4\frac{1}{2} + (-6\frac{1}{2})$
3. $\frac{1}{2} + (-\frac{1}{4})$ **6.** $4\frac{1}{4} + (-5)$ **9.** $-1\frac{1}{2} + 2\frac{1}{8}$

RATIONAL NUMBERS 11.5, PAGE 42.

1. $-\frac{1}{2}$ **6.** $-\frac{17}{21}$ **11.** $9\frac{1}{3}$
2. 0 **7.** $-\frac{1}{5}$ **12.** $-1\frac{1}{6}$
3. $-\frac{11}{16}$ **8.** $\frac{3}{8}$ **13.** 4
4. $-\frac{2}{3}$ **9.** $-\frac{3}{8}$ **14.** $-5\frac{17}{24}$
5. $-\frac{5}{8}$ **10.** $-9\frac{5}{8}$ **15.** $-2\frac{5}{14}$

Rational Numbers 11.6, page 42.

1. $y = \frac{8}{35}$
2. $x = -3\frac{4}{5}$
3. $z = 5\frac{1}{2}$
4. $a = -9\frac{1}{8}$
5. $m = 3\frac{1}{6}$
6. $n = 6\frac{1}{4}$
7. $s = 6\frac{3}{8}$
8. $w = -\frac{7}{10}$
9. $t = -3\frac{27}{40}$
10. $v = 2\frac{37}{40}$
11. $d = -5\frac{1}{2}$
12. $e = -10\frac{7}{16}$
13. $g = -1\frac{5}{6}$
14. $h = -3\frac{1}{16}$
15. $k = -8\frac{5}{8}$

Rational Numbers 11.7, page 44.

1. $-, -\frac{1}{4}$
2. $-, -2$
3. $-, -\frac{1}{16}$
4. $+, 8\frac{65}{128}$
5. $+, 2\frac{1}{3}$
6. $+, 26\frac{1}{4}$
7. $-, -28\frac{1}{3}$
8. $-, -1$
9. $-, -1$
10. $+, 5\frac{5}{14}$
11. $+, \frac{5}{6}$
12. $+, 25\frac{5}{6}$

Rational Numbers 11.8, page 44.

1. $y = -1\frac{2}{3}$
2. $w = -1\frac{2}{3}$
3. $z = \frac{1}{28}$
4. $v = \frac{1}{3}$
5. $s = -\frac{7}{12}$
6. $r = 1\frac{3}{4}$
7. $p = -7\frac{7}{12}$
8. $m = 19\frac{1}{4}$
9. $a = 1\frac{13}{32}$
10. $b = 6$
11. $c = -21\frac{8}{15}$
12. $d = 11\frac{1}{9}$
13. $g = -2\frac{1}{4}$
14. $h = 16\frac{1}{2}$
15. $k = -1$
16. $f = -\frac{13}{30}$
17. $n = 14\frac{2}{3}$
18. $x = -12\frac{1}{2}$

Rational Numbers 11.9, page 46.

1. $+, x = 1\frac{7}{8}$
2. $-, \frac{5}{6}$
3. $-, \frac{3}{28}$
4. $-, m = \frac{1}{15}$
5. $-, 2\frac{1}{10}$
6. $+, 3\frac{7}{15}$
7. $-, y = 28\frac{4}{5}$
8. $+, 1$
9. $-, z = 8$

Rational Numbers 11.10, page 46.

1. $a = 3$
2. $r = -56$
3. $t = -\frac{1}{10}$
4. $s = 1\frac{17}{28}$
5. $v = 2\frac{13}{14}$
6. $w = -14$
7. $x = -1\frac{5}{16}$
8. $y = 1\frac{1}{15}$
9. $z = -5\frac{5}{12}$
10. $c = 1\frac{3}{10}$
11. $d = 1\frac{9}{16}$
12. $e = 7\frac{7}{8}$
13. $g = -7\frac{1}{9}$
14. $h = 3\frac{2}{7}$
15. $j = 2$

Ratio, Proportion, and Percent 12.1, page 47.

1. $\frac{4}{5}$
2. $\frac{49}{50}$
3. $\frac{5}{11}$
4. $\frac{2}{3}$
5. $\frac{3}{5}$
6. $\frac{24}{1}$
7. $\frac{5}{73}$
8. $\frac{2}{5}$
9. $\frac{1}{8}$

Ratio, Proportion, and Percent 12.2, page 48.

1. $\frac{1}{3}$
2. $\frac{3}{2}$
3. $\frac{1}{4}$
4. $\frac{2}{1}$
5. $\frac{1}{2}$
6. $\frac{3}{5}$

Ratio, Proportion, and Percent 12.3, page 48.

1. $a = 6$
2. $b = 2$
3. $c = 5$
4. $d = 6$
5. $e = 5$
6. $f = 4; g = 5$
7. $h = 12; j = 5$
8. $k = 9; m = 2$
9. $n = 4; p = 3$
10. $r = 6; s = 4$
11. $t = 7; v = 2$
12. $w = 11; x = 11; z = 2$
13. $y = 18$
14. $x = 40$
15. $a = 36$

Ratio, Proportion, and Percent 12.4, page 48.

1. $a = 21; b = 7$
2. $e = 15; f = 25$
3. $g = 6$
4. $h = 3$
5. $j = 15; k = 15$
6. $m = 13; n = 104$
7. $p = 4; q = 4$
8. $r = 11; s = 11$
9. $t = 6; u = 42$
10. $v = 4; w = 28$
11. $x = 4; y = 4; z = 48$
12. $a = 10; b = 10; c = 240$

Ratio, Proportion, and Percent 12.5, page 49.

1. $=$
2. $\neq$
3. $\neq$
4. $=$
5. $\neq$
6. $=$
7. $=$
8. $\neq$
9. $\neq$
10. $=$
11. $\neq$
12. $\neq$
13. $=$
14. $\neq$
15. $\neq$

Ratio, Proportion, and Percent 12.6, page 50.

1. $b = 9$
2. $c = 6$
3. $m = 7$
4. $c = 3$
5. $x = 33$
6. $w = 3$
7. $h = 128$
8. $d = 54$
9. $a = 132$
10. $v = 26$
11. $t = 6$
12. $e = 15$

Ratio, Proportion, and Percent 12.7, page 51.

1. 5.24%
2. 140%
3. 300%
4. 496.2%
5. 6258%
6. .32%
7. 770%
8. neither

Ratio, Proportion, and Percent 12.8, page 51.

1. .68
2. .01
3. .05367
4. .096
5. .06
6. 70
7. .999
8. .0006
9. .5274
10. .009
11. .4622
12. .298
13. .00027
14. 14.67
15. 1.76

Ratio, Proportion, and Percent 12.9, page 52.

1. 10%
2. 50%
3. 11.1%
4. 12.5%
5. 5%
6. 187.5%
7. 431%
8. 80%
9. 650%
10. 914.3%
11. 65%
12. 133.3%
13. 666.7%
14. 38.9%
15. 136.7%

Ratio, Proportion, and Percent 12.10, page 52.

1. $\frac{11}{20}$
2. $\frac{1}{50}$
3. $14\frac{3}{10}$
4. $\frac{3}{5}$
5. $\frac{3}{4}$
6. $\frac{57}{100}$
7. $1\frac{1}{5}$
8. $\frac{19}{20}$
9. $\frac{4}{5}$
10. $2\frac{1}{2}$
11. $3\frac{1}{4}$
12. $\frac{81}{100}$
13. 7
14. $\frac{1}{20}$
15. $\frac{1}{8}$

Ratio, Proportion, and Percent 12.11, page 53.

1. 25% $\frac{1}{4}$ .25
2. 37% $\frac{37}{100}$ .37
3. 6% $\frac{3}{50}$ .06
4. 12.5% $\frac{1}{8}$ .125
5. 32% $\frac{8}{25}$ .32
6. 50% $\frac{1}{2}$ .5
7. 80% $\frac{4}{5}$ .8
8. 39% $\frac{39}{100}$ .39

9.	64%	$\frac{16}{25}$	.64	15.	2%	$\frac{1}{50}$	.02
10.	220%	$2\frac{1}{5}$	2.2	16.	1000%	$\frac{10}{1}$	10
11.	1%	$\frac{1}{100}$	.01	17.	20%	$\frac{1}{5}$	.2
12.	575%	$5\frac{3}{4}$	5.75	18.	700%	7	7
13.	4.5%	$\frac{9}{200}$	.045	19.	45%	$\frac{9}{200}$	.45
14.	12.5%	$\frac{1}{8}$	.125	20.	90%	$\frac{9}{10}$	.9

65.	$5\frac{3}{4}$	5.75	575%
66.	$\frac{1}{500}$	.002	.2%
67.	$\frac{9}{200}$	.045	4.5%
68.	$\frac{1}{20}$	.05	5%
69.	$\frac{9}{20}$	.45	45%
70.	$\frac{877}{1000}$ or $\frac{87.7}{100}$	.877	87.7%

MASTERY TEST, PAGE 54.

A. Factors

1. 8: 2, 4   **3.** 19: 19   **5.** 45: 3, 9
2. 20: 10, 20   **4.** 28: 7   **6.** 22: 1, 2

B. Composite Numbers

7. 2•2•3•7   **8.** 2•3•3•5   **9.** 2•2•2•2•2•2

C. Greatest Common Factor & Lowest Common Multiple

10. GCF=6 LMC=36 **12.** GCF=6 LMC=72 **14.** GCF=3 LMC=252
11. GCF=15 LMC=90 **13.** GCF=2 LMC=132 **15.** GCF=4 LMC=400

D. Simplify Exponetial Expressons

16. 9^3 **19.** y^{12} **22.** $13y^2$
17. 5^2 **20.** 1   **23.** $10b^5$
18. 10^5 **21.** a   **24.** $5c^3$

E. Variables and Order

25. wxy   **29.** 8cd   **33.** 5m÷n
26. 6   **30.** $64k^2+5$ **34.** 23w+17x+y+7
27. 56rst   **31.** v÷w   **35.** 14p–15q
28. 27g–6   **32.** 12xy   **36.** 84c

F. Properties
  (answers may vary)

37. 12+6+y=6+12+y
        18y=18y

38. 27•(4•5)=(27•4)•5
        540=540

39. 3(4+7–8)=3(4) +3(7)–3(8)
        9=9

40. a. Distributive   **b.** Associative   **c.** Commutative

G. Integers with Rational Numbers

41. –16   **45.** b = –3   **49.** $-\frac{7}{8}$
42. x = 89   **46.** m = –297   **50.** –4
43. 89   **47.** $\frac{1}{3}$ **51.** $z = -1\frac{11}{12}$
44. $-\frac{1}{5}$ **48.** $a = -10\frac{5}{6}$ **52.** 60

H. Ratio, Proportion and Percent

53. 451%   **55.** 12.5%   **57.** 38.9%
54. 467%   **56.** 187.5%   **58.** 10%

59. 2.78%   **61.** 452%   **63.** 90%
60. 700%   **62.** .6%   **64.** 38.4%

Errata Sheet
corrections

Our apology. Please find corrections to the Answer pages.

PRIME AND COMPOSITE NUMBERS 3.2, PAGE 11.

1. 81=3•3•3•3   **8.** 39=3•13   **15.** 144=2•2•2•2•3•3
2. 48=2•2•2•2•3   **9.** 90=2•3•3•5 **16.** 84=2•2•3•7
3. 225=3•3•5•5   **10.** 88=2•2•2•11 **17.** 430=2•5•43
4. 64=2•2•2•2•2•2 **11.** 225=3•3•5•5 **18.** 248=2•2•2•31
5. 14=2•7   **12.** 48=2•2•2•2•3 **19.** 137=1•137
6. 21=3•7   **13.** 126=2•3•3•7 **20.** 91=7•13
7. 35=5•7   **14.** 46=2•23

VARIABLES 7.5, PAGE 23.
  17. $81s^2+5$
INTEGERS 9.8, PAGE 30.
  16. +
INTEGERS 9.9, PAGE 30.
  16. 143
INTEGEPS 9.11, PAGE 31.
  3. –
INTEGERS 9.12, PAGE 31.
  3. –108
INTEGERS 9.13, PAGE 31.
  8. m = –81
MORE WITH EXPONENTS, PAGE 38.
  5. $150x^6$

Math Series

The Straight Forward Math Series

is systematic, first diagnosing skill levels, then *practice*, periodic *review*, and *testing*.

Blackline

GP-006 Addition
GP-012 Subtraction
GP-007 Multiplication
GP-013 Division
GP-039 Fractions
GP-083 Word Problems, Book 1
GP-042 Word Problems, Book 2

GarlicPress
Tools for Learning and Growing

The Advanced Straight Forward Math Series

is a higher level system to diagnose, practice, review, and test skills.

Blackline

GP-015 Advanced Addition
GP-016 Advanced Subtraction
GP-017 Advanced Multiplication
GP-018 Advanced Division
GP-020 Advanced Decimals
GP-021 Advanced Fractions
GP-044 Mastery Tests
GP-025 Percent
GP-028 Pre-Algebra, Book 1
GP-029 Pre-Algebra, Book 2
GP-030 Pre-Geometry, Book 1
GP-031 Pre-Geometry, Book 2

Upper Level Math Series

GP-104 Algebra, Book 1
GP-105 Algebra, Book 2
GP-045 Trigonometry
GP-054 Geometry
GP-053 Pre-Calculus
GP-064 Calculus AB, Vol. 1
GP-067 Calculus AB, Vol. 2

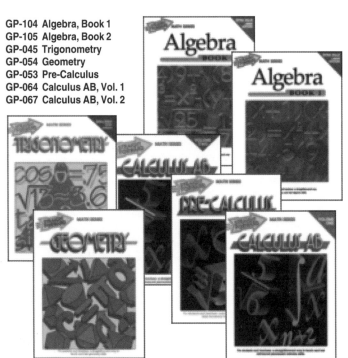

2 SIDED Self-Checking Math Puzzles

Each puzzle set contains 10 individual puzzles. Each six-inch puzzle is two-sided. One side contains basic math facts, the other side has a photograph. Each puzzle has its own clear plastic tray and lid.

Math problems are solved in the bottom tray (answer pieces are all the same shape). The lid is closed and the puzzle is turned over. If the photo is jumbled, the math facts have not been completed correctly.

GP-113 Addition Puzzles
GP-114 Subtraction Puzzles
GP-115 Multiplication Puzzles
GP-116 Division Puzzles
GP-122 Multiplication & Division Puzzles
GP-123 Money Puzzles

front puzzle   back photo